Smoothies

Eliq Maranik

Smoothies

REFRESHING, HEALTHY, AND DELICIOUS

h.f.**ullmann**

CONTENTS

INTRODUCTION

I hope this book will inspire you and make you as fascinated by composing your own smoothies as I am. You will learn what fruits go together, when and how to buy them, and how to prepare them before use. The more you know about it, the more fun it gets!

The way food and drink is presented is enormously important to me. Eating should be a feast for all the senses. Since I am passionate about color and form, I have chosen glasses and made, designed, and photographed all these wonderful drinks with that in mind. Feel free to adapt the recipes according to your own taste or to what you happen to have at home at the moment. I hope this book will inspire you to invent new, delicious combinations, and that many of these recipes will become some of your favorites.

This book is a guide to the process of choosing fruit, berries, and vegetables, and it also contains some brief facts about them. You will learn how to prepare and freeze the produce and about useful tools and utensils. The difference between organically grown and regular produce is explained and there are serving and garnishing suggestions as well as other useful information.

The main section includes 100 amazing smoothie recipes divided into four categories: Fruit and Berry Smoothies, Yogurt & Breakfast Smoothies, Vegetable Smoothies, and Dessert Smoothies. The final chapter is dedicated to some less healthy, but oh so delicious, cocktails made from fresh fruit and berries.

These recipes are predominantly made from our most common fruits and vegetables, but lots of other wholesome ingredients can be added. I give some brief suggestions in the chapter on ingredients. For a more substantial smoothie you may, for example, add fiber, nuts, super berries, powdered berries, nourishing oils, or protein powder. If you suffer from any health problems, do ask at your nearest health food shop whether there is anything you should avoid.

Best of luck!

Eliq Maranik

GETTING STARTED

Choose Your Vegetables, Fruits, and Berries Carefully!

Making the right shopping decisions is essential when you are making smoothies—you need to learn to find, select, store, and use seasonal produce in the proper way.

Most important when it comes to finding the very best fruits and vegetables, however, is to use your eyes, nose, and hands, and to look for organically grown produce. The freshest produce is to be found at your local market or farm shop. You can be sure that nothing you buy there has been harvested before it is ripe in order to survive transportation over long distances. Moreover, prices tend to be more affordable than in the main street.

Take your time, and only buy as much as you are likely to consume within the next few days. Do not stockpile fruits and vegetables unless you are planning to freeze them first. Storage reduces the quality of all fresh produce.

Look for firm, fragrant fruits with a healthy color and without soft, blemished, or discolored parts. Picking out your own is better than buying packaged fruit and vegetables, which are harder to assess.

It is also important to store fruits and vegetables in a place where they will keep well. Remember that some fruits and vegetables should not be kept close together. Tests have shown that many fruits and vegetables that are sold in shops contain pesticide residues—choose organically grown produce that is free from additives and pesticides, have softer skins, and are superior in flavor. Organically grown produce is a little dearer to buy, but is definitely worth the expense. Compare organically and conventionally grown varieties to discover the difference and your personal favorites. I keep a log, which is very useful. Unfortunately, the names of mangos, oranges, etc. are not always displayed on the shelf. If the name is not shown, ask! If the staff are unable to answer, find out who can. Someone ought to know since this is the kind of information that should be supplied on delivery.

There are companies that deliver fruits and vegetables to your door. These will provide information on the country of origin and name of what you are buying, and sometimes even the name of the grower.

The single most important factor when making smoothies is choosing the right ingredients. Smoothies and juices are no better than the fruits and vegetables from which you make them. The better the ingredients, the better the end result. Choose fruits and vegetables in season for the best result. Fresh fruit has an intense flavor and tastes delicious, while fruit that was harvested some time ago, before it was ripe, and then transported over long distances, is often watery and tasteless. Juices and smoothies can be made from virtually any fruits or vegetables as long as they are properly prepared.

Ripe or Unripe?

Choose fruits that are just ripe for the best flavor and texture. Unripe fruit is more acidic, harder, and lacks that special flavor. Overripe fruit often tastes too sweet, bad even, and the smoothie will become sickly—the flavors become more intense during maceration or juicing. Overripe fruit such as bananas, peaches, or mangos will spoil your smoothie. Choose fragrant fruits that feel heavy in comparison to their size—it is usually a sign of ripeness.

Most fruits ripen at room temperature after being harvested. Some become sweeter and juicier with storage, others become juicier but not sweeter. Citrus fruits are one of the few exceptions. They do not continue to ripen after picking, but they can become juicier by being left out in the kitchen.

Wash all Fruits, Berries, and Vegetables

Unless you pick the fruit and vegetables in your own garden, you have no idea how they have been treated in storage and who has touched them, not to mention the amount of pesticides that have been used. Most of them, especially imported fruits and vegetables, are sprayed in order to keep them longer. This is why it is extremely important that you wash and scrub everything carefully and peel anything that has not been organically grown. Anything present on the surface will otherwise end up inside your body.

It is easiest to wash all hard fruits and vegetables in lukewarm water, using a soft brush that should be used only for this purpose and then properly cleaned afterwards. Rinse soft fruit in lukewarm or hot water and rub them or use the soft side of a scourer kept only for that purpose. Use a small amount of dishwashing liquid and a soft sponge to clean citrus fruits and waxed fruits. Remember always to rinse the fruit properly after using detergents.

You can buy special organic detergents for cleaning fruit. They remove wax and dirt from the surface. Instead, squeeze half a lemon into the lukewarm water and soak the fruit for 20 seconds before scrubbing. If the wax is hard to remove, you can use dish-washing liquid first and then continue with the above method. Peel all fruit that has not been organically grown to be on the safe side.

Even fruit with peels that are not eaten—bananas, oranges, mandarins, melons, and mangos, for example, should be cleaned properly since pesticides and waxes adhere to your hands and will end up in your smoothie when you touch the pulp.

To Peel or Not to Peel?

Most of the vitamins, minerals, and enzymes in the fruit are found just underneath or in the peel, which is why it is preferable not to peel the fruit. You do not normally have to peel organically grown produce, but wash all fruits, berries, and vegetables properly in warm water before eating. If you are not using organic produce, I recommend that you always peel off the outermost layer of the skin. Always peel bananas, mangos, pineapples, papayas, and avocados. Kiwi does not always need to be peeled. You can leave the skin if you are passing it through a juicer, but if you are using a blender, you are advised to peel it. Leave the peel on unwaxed citrus fruits if you are chopping or zesting it. If you are using a citrus press, you should of course not peel the fruit. It is normally best to avoid hard peels and seeds in your smoothies since these tend to make them lumpy.

Removing Pits and Seeds

Remove pits from nectarines, peaches, plums, apricots, mangos, avocados, and other stone fruit. Soft pits and seeds can be passed through a juicer or blender, but I normally remove them since they add flavor and affect the texture. Dark seeds from, for example, watermelon or passion fruit may affect the color, so try and remove them beforehand. Always remove papaya seeds as they will ruin the flavor.

Preparation and Freezing

Prepare all fruits, berries, and vegetables before use. Many nutrients, vitamins, minerals, and enzymes oxidize soon after you cut the fruit. If you buy a lot of fruit in season, prepare it, pack it in plastic bags, and freeze immediately. Even though fresh produce is always best, produce that has been frozen immediately after harvesting is preferable to fruit that is not ripe or has been stored. Strawberries, raspberries, and blueberries keep for only a few days, so always prepare and freeze them immediately unless you are using them straight away.

If you make a lot of smoothies, you should bulk buy fruit in season. Always write the date, number of portions, and contents on the freezer bags. Prepare the fruit as if you were using it to make a smoothie, and pack in batches of one or several types of fruits and berries. Fruit keeps well for 2–3 months in an ordinary freezer, but can be kept longer in temperatures below 0 ºF/-18 ºC. In shops and storage facilities, the temperature is usually at that level or lower, which is colder than your freezer at home. You should preferably use resealable bags that keep the air out. Try and press out as much air as possible before sealing.

The best method for freezing berries is to pour a small amount at a time on the bottom of a small baking sheet and then freeze until they are solid. Then transfer to a freezer bag to prevent them from turning into pulp. Juicy fruits can be prepared in the same way.

When you make smoothies, pour the frozen fruit or berries straight into the blender, mix them with the liquid, or thaw before use. It is a good idea to thaw frozen berries if you are using a juicer, as they will not yield any juice when frozen.

Using a Juicer

You get more out of hard fruits and vegetables if you extract the juices before adding them to the blender. It is easiest to use a juicer. Note that no juice can be extracted from bananas or avocados; they need to be mashed or puréed in the blender.

Using a Blender

Soft fruit such as stone fruits, berries, and tropical fruits are perfect for blending into smooth and juicy purées without any of the nutritional value being lost. Harder fruits (e.g. apples and pears) that produce dense, fibrous smoothies should preferably be juiced before being added to the blender.

Always Clean the Juicer After Use

Always clean your appliances with the help of a soft brush immediately after use. It will help extend the life of expensive juicers and blenders.

Organically Grown Produce

Organically grown fruits, vegetables, and berries are harvested when they are almost ripe. It means that they have lower water content and a better aroma, they taste better, and they are juicier and better for you than conventionally grown fruit. On the other hand, they do not keep as well, they are more sensitive, and they may have more blemishes and bruises than conventionally grown produce since no preservatives, additives, pesticides, or waxes have been added to prolong their life, make them look shiny, and help them keep their shape. Organically grown fruit should be kept in a dark, cool place and consumed as soon as possible. Normally, you do not need to peel organically grown fruits; simply scrub them in lukewarm, running water. Organic vegetables contain more vitamins, minerals, enzymes, and other nutrients than conventionally grown produce. They have high vitamin C levels and contain antioxidants—e.g. vitamin E and carotenoids—that protect the cells in our bodies against cardiac and vascular disease.

Ethylene Gas

It may be useful to know that some fruits and vegetables produce ethylene gas, which speeds up the ripening process—partly for the fruit itself, but also for other fruits and vegetables close by. Apples, pears, melons, bananas, peaches, nectarines, plums, apricots, and tomatoes contain high levels and should not be kept with other fruits and vegetables since these may become shrivelled, go off, or become overripe. Carrots can become bitter, cucumbers become shrivelled; and bananas, mangos, and avocados ripen too quickly if they are stored too close to other ethylene-producing fruits. But you can use them to make other fruits ripen faster. Just place them in the same bowl or bag. Examples of vegetables that do not tolerate ethylene gas well are cucumbers, squash, dill, carrots, lettuce, leeks, and zucchini. These should be kept separately.

Use Your Creativity

Do not be afraid of composing your own recipes, but remember not to mix too many different types of fruit; mild juices made from apples, pears, carrots, and oranges go well with most other fruits and vegetables, but avoid mixing too many strong flavors. If you are using vegetables with a strong or bitter taste, you can always dilute and sweeten them by using the above mentioned juices. You do not normally associate smoothies with vegetables, but they can be used sparingly. Try making smoothies from beet, chilli, spinach, celery, bell pepper, or broccoli juice, or simply drink it neat. Experiment with spices, powdered berries, algae, nuts, seeds, protein powder, dried berries, or natural fibers. Do not forget the garnish. Use your imagination!

Why Make Your Own Smoothies and Juices?

The answer is simple: it is fun, it is simple, it is good, and my body likes it! Last time I went shopping I noticed many different readymade smoothies and juices, and new ones are constantly added as we grow increasingly aware of what we eat, that vitamins and minerals are important, and that our stomachs need natural fiber. And I am not talking about the manufactured fiber you add to your food, but the natural fiber found in fruits, vegetables, and grains. Now that all these products are so readily available, why should you make life more difficult by investing in a whole range of appliances that are difficult to clean, carry home heavy bags of fruit, and spend time preparing them?

The advantage of making your own juices and mixing smoothies from fresh or thawed fruits, berries, and vegetables is that you always know exactly what is in them. You can pick your favorite ingredients and make sure you always buy the freshest and best ingredients available. Moreover, you can easily adapt the proportions and your favorite flavors. The choices are limitless, and it is hard to stop once you have become used to it.

Always try to buy fruit and vegetables that are in season—it is cheaper and they are more nutritious. Seasonal produce can always be frozen and used out of season.

Smoothies and juices are becoming increasingly popular in cafés; it is great to be able to find alternatives to lattes and desserts, but do ask how and where the ingredients were grown, and watch your smoothie being made. Do not hesitate to ask about the contents and when the fruit was prepared when you are buying a readymade smoothie since flavor, nutritional value, and appearance change soon after it is made. It is best of all when you are actually able to watch the fruit being prepared.

Commercial Brands

Today, there are many serious and committed commercial smoothie brands, suitable for those who neither have the time nor the inclination to make their own. These are usually made from 100% fruits without additives, flavor enhancers, colorings, sweeteners, or concentrated fruit juices. However, they are pasteurized in order to keep them for as long as up to a week and, unfortunately, with the removal of harmful bacteria, much of the original goodness is lost.

These smoothies are without a doubt a perfectly good alternative, but they cannot compete with a freshly made smoothie made from fresh fruit, cut immediately before going into the machine, and drunk straight away. Watch out for smoothies that contain colorings, flavor enhancers, sweeteners, concentrates, and other additives. The label should list nothing except fruit.

Serving and Garnishing

It is important to me that whatever I am about to eat or drink appears appetizing to all my senses. That is why I prefer to serve my smoothies in pretty glasses and garnish them with fresh berries, fruits, vegetables, herbs, edible flowers, or anything else I can find in the kitchen. There are infinite ways of garnishing and serving a smoothie or fruit juice—it is rather like serving cocktails that are even more famous because of their fantastic decorations and amusing decor. Using various types of ice is another way of adding something extra. Look for ice trays and bags with unusual shapes, or freeze berries, edible flowers, and herbs in ice cubes for an extravagant, surprising touch. I save all the fun cocktail sticks I can find for later use when I am traveling. DIY stores offer many ideas. Instead, involve the whole family and make your own decorations. Each drink should be impossible to resist. Children, who are often hard to convince, will love it and they will discover that smoothies are cool, especially if they are allowed to shop for ingredients and help with making them. Invite children and adult friends to freeze their smoothies in ice-cream molds with a stick so they can eat them on a hot summer day. But do not keep frozen smoothie ice cream in the freezer for too long as it will lose its flavor and texture.

As you will see from my recipes, I love to vary my smoothies as much as possible by using different types of glass, flavors, and garnishes.

TOOLS

All you need to make a smoothie is a sharp knife and an electric blender or an immersion blender and beaker. However, there are a number of other tools and appliances that can help speed up the process and make variation easier.

A BLENDER is essential for making smoothies. If you do not have one, use an immersion blender and beaker, but a real blender is more fun. Simply place all the ingredients in the container, press the button, and pour the smoothie into a glass.

When you are choosing your blender, consider motor capacity, speed, volume, and if it crushes ice. I recommend one with a glass container since they are more robust and hygienic, and do not get scratched and discolored as easily as plastic ones. Crushing ice is not essential, but it helps.

A JUICER. If you intend to make juice from vegetables and hard fruits, you will need a proper juicer that extracts the juice from everything from hard root vegetables to soft berries. There are two types: centrifugal juicers and masticating juicers. Remember that different machines perform in different ways and extract more or less juice from whatever you feed into them. I recommend you compare brands before making a decision. If pressing juice is what you are after, you should invest in a masticating juicer (see below).

A CENTRIFUGAL JUICER processes fruits and vegetables and extracts the juice by pushing the pulp through a fine mesh. These appliances are often less expensive, but produce less juice than a masticating juicer. Moreover, some enzymes are killed because the rotating blades become hot during processing. It causes the juice to oxidize, which means that it does not keep as well as juices that have been extracted in

a masticating juicer. Centrifuged juices should preferably be consumed immediately or within 24 hours. It is important that you clean the centrifugal juicer immediately after use since it is hard to remove encrusted pulp. Use the brush provided.

A MASTICATING JUICER masticates the fruits and vegetables and forces the pulp through a fine metal mesh. They are a little more expensive, but more efficient, and they can deal with larger quantities. Masticating juicers come in different price categories, so think carefully before you make up your mind. The nutritional value of the juice extracted is higher and it retains more of the important enzymes compared to juice made in a centrifugal juicer. The juice should be consumed immediately or within 48 hours. The appliance should be cleaned immediately to prevent the pulp from drying and adhering to the different parts of the machine.

A CITRUS JUICE EXTRACTOR is a very useful appliance. There are many different types, both electric and manual. It is the amount of juice you plan to make that determines the type you need. If you are making one or two glasses at a time, an ordinary, manual juice extractor suffices; they are easy to clean and take up little space. They are also relatively inexpensive. If you are planning to make large quantities, it may be worth investing in a more advanced manual or electric extractor. It must be cleaned immediately after use since it is hard to clean once the pulp has dried.

AN IMMERSION BLENDER is an excellent choice for small quantities. It is easy to use and to clean. Do not use it with ice, since the blades are easily damaged. Immersion blenders are intended for mashing food, not for crushing frozen fruits or ice.

A FOOD PROCESSOR is a useful appliance, but it is more suitable for making large quantities. Since food processors are made up of many small parts, they are more difficult to clean and pour from, and there is a lot of waste since there is always something left in the bowl.

CUTTING BOARD. Always use separate cutting boards for fruits and vegetables. Clean them immediately after use since they may become discolored and absorb aromas. Even if you clean them well, they trap bacteria, so use separate cutting boards for meat, fish, and vegetables.

BRUSHES, hard and soft, are useful since many vitamins, antioxidants, fibers, and minerals are in or just underneath the peel. Carrots, beets, and other hard root vegetables need to be scrubbed properly, while soft fruit such as ripe pears and kiwis need a lighter touch.

If you are using organic, locally grown fruit you may not need to peel it, but always wash it to be on the safe side and if you do peel, remove as thin a layer as possible. Waxes and pesticide residues are extremely hard to remove. It may be wise to peel all fruit in order to avoid ingesting toxins that could be harmful in the long term. You can buy special fruit cleaning agents that dissolve waxes and other residues.

A POTATO PEELER is invaluable. Use it to peel mangos, root vegetables and, for example, pears that are not organically grown. Remember to wash the fruit before you peel it.

COLANDERS AND SIEVES. You can easily achieve a very smooth result by passing the fruit through a fine mesh to prevent all the bits of peel, seeds, pits, and other unwanted parts from ending up in your glass. I normally pass orange, grapefruit, lemon, and lime juice through a sieve so that the seeds do not spoil my smoothies and juices. Use a nylon sieve for acid fruit; metal may affect the flavor.

KITCHEN SCALES are very useful when measuring berries, but remember that fruits and berries taste differently depending on season and type, so a small amount extra here or there makes no difference when you are making a smoothie. What is important is that you enjoy it and learn to experiment with flavors.

AN OLIVE PITTER is very useful for pitting cherries and other small stone fruit. If you do not have one at home use a small pointed knife, but a proper olive pitter is best.

AN APPLE CORER makes life easier if you cannot be bothered to quarter and core apples and pears with a knife. You end up with a nice, whole fruit you can use for garnishing.

AN ORANGE PEELER produces thicker, longer peels than a zester, but you can achieve the same result with a knife.

A SPATULA made of soft silicon saves waste and is useful for scraping the last drops out of the blender container.

KNIVES—large and small. I recommend high-quality, stainless steel knives. Always use large knives for large fruits so you can cut perfect slices without losing a finger. Use a small knife for cutting decorations from peels and entire fruits. Use your imagination. The sharper, thinner, and more flexible the knife, the easier it is to remove pith and membranes from grapefruits, oranges, and other citrus fruit, or to cut wafer thin slices from kiwis. Since all the nutrients are in or immediately underneath the skin, the less you remove the better it is.

MEASURES of various sizes are important for measuring thawed berries and fruits, milk, juice, yogurt, spices, sugar, and other ingredients. But a good eye goes a long way too.

AN ICE CREAM SCOOP is useful for ice-cream-based smoothies. Ordinary tablespoons may bend while ice cream scoops are made from a more robust material that can deal with hard, frozen ice cream, sorbets, or frozen yogurts without breaking. Dip it in warm water before and in between scoops.

A GRATER is very useful for grating citrus peel, ginger, carrots, beets, or anything else you may want to grate before putting it in the blender, or to make decorations. Use a stainless steel one if you are grating acid fruits or citrus fruits.

FREEZER BAGS are my best friends and indispensable for freezing berries, fruits, herbs, etc. They are the most economic and hygienic way of freezing fruits and berries. I always buy large quantities of fruits and berries in season. Then I prepare them and freeze them in batches. I recommend you label your bags. Use resealable plastic bags if you can get them.

LABELS. It is a good idea to label your bags of frozen fruits, berries, yogurt cubes, and juice cubes with information about content, date, and number of batches or weight.

ICE CUBE TRAYS/MOLDS. Buy plenty of different types of chocolate molds and ice cube trays for freezing water, fruit juice, ice cream, or yogurt. Put a few berries, edible flowers, or herbs inside the ice cubes, or fill the molds with passion fruit pulp, fruit juice, or smoothie mixture for instant access.

AN ICE CRUSHER is not essential. Most blenders can deal with a few ice cubes. Alternatively, place the ice in a clean towel and use a heavy object or a hammer to crush it.

FREEZER. A large freezer is very useful for keeping large quantities of berries and fruits, ice cubes, or smoothies. Fruits and berries should not be kept for more than 2–3 months in an ordinary freezer. They keep longer in temperatures below 0 °F/-18 °C.

REFRIGERATORS. All dairy products must of course be kept refrigerated, but most fruits too need to be kept cool, preferably in a sealed plastic bag, to avoid becoming overripe or ruined by other foodstuffs. If you want it to ripen quickly, leave it out at room temperature.

TIPS AND ADVICE

Tone Down Flavors

Some fruits and vegetables have a strong flavor. These should be used sparingly and mixed with milder fruits and vegetables. For example, if you use a lot of chilli and ginger, your smoothie will be undrinkable. Use small quantities and combine with milder juices. If you discover that a flavor has spoilt the taste, add some carrot, apple, pear, or orange juice.

Flavor Enhancers

If you find the result is too bland, you can add a little lemon or lime juice, it brings out the other flavors. Some fruits—melon, mango, and banana, for example—can turn out a little too sweet. Simply add a little citrus juice to bring out their fruitiness.

Thinner Smoothies

If your smoothie turns out too thick or more like a purée than a liquid—e.g. if you have used fruits with too little water content—you can dilute it with a little water, milk, buttermilk, or juice. Water is the best if you do not want to lose any of the fruity character.

Thicker Smoothies

If your smoothie is a bit too thin you can add a little crème fraîche, quark, Greek yogurt, banana, avocado, or mango. For an even creamier result, use ice cream or cream; or add some tofu, muesli, nuts, or other goodies.

Smoother Smoothies

Some fruits and vegetables are very rich in fiber and make the smoothie thick and hard to drink (e.g. pineapple, pear, and apple). If that is the case you can juice or purée the fruits before adding them to the smoothie. Extract the juice by pressing it through a fine mesh and return it to the blender with the rest of the ingredients.

Frozen Smoothies

Add plenty of ice for a refreshing summer smoothie or juice. Remember that the ice melts quickly and ruins the taste if the smoothie is too warm to start with, so you could cool the fruit before preparing it to keep the flavors fresh. Remember that it is better to use too much ice than too little. A small amount of ice melts quickly and you end up with a smoothie full of water. Another tip is to cool the smoothie or juice before turning it into a sorbet or frozen smoothie by mixing in the ice.

Serve Immediately

In order to make the most of the vitamins, flavors, colors, and texture you must serve all smoothies and juices as soon as possible after preparation. If you want to save it for later, keep it in mind that it needs to be kept in a clean, sealed glass container in the fridge—preferably no longer than 24 hours since the vitamins begin to disappear straight after the fruit is pressed, and smoothies go bad rather quickly. Home-made smoothies change color and taste fairly quickly, so I recommend you consume them immediately. Always shake the smoothie before you drink it and serve with attractive berries or sliced fruit to please the eye.

FRUITS, BERRIES, AND VEGETABLES

APPLES contain plenty of antioxidants and vitamin C. They are a good source of natural fiber, which contributes to lowering cholesterol levels in the blood. Apples should be kept cool, preferably refrigerated, in plastic bags. They do not keep well at room temperature. Apples produce ethylene gas, which speeds up the ripening process. Stock up on local varieties during the fall; they are the best. Apples can be frozen after they have been cut into wedges and the cores and seeds removed.

APRICOTS resemble plums, but have a yellowish, furry skin. They contain beta-carotene, which is converted to vitamin A. They also contain a lot of fiber, potassium, and vitamin C. The fruits can be left out at room temperature for one or a couple of days, but are best kept at 32 °F/0 °C. Apricots are often imported to northern Europe from the Mediterranean region in the summer and from South America in the winter.

AVOCADOS are the fruit of the avocado tree and an excellent source of vitamin E. Buy hard, unripe avocados and keep them at room temperature for 3–4 days. The process can be speeded up by placing the avocados in a paper or plastic bag together with an apple, pear, or banana. Ripe avocados keep for about three days in a plastic bag in the refrigerator. An avocado is ripe when the flesh is spongy and yields to light pressure. It keeps well in the fridge at home, but will form dark spots and remain hard if the temperature is too low. Avocados are primarily cultivated in Spain, Mexico, and Israel.

BANANAS are usually sold when they are still green and unripe, and they ripen in contact with other fruits that emit ethylene gas, which speeds up the process. Bananas contain high levels of potassium, vitamin B6, and magnesium. Do not store bananas in the refrigerator or they will turn black. Always keep them at room temperature, preferably in a separate bowl away from other fruits because of the ethylene gas. Bananas can make other fruits ripen faster. They are delicate and quickly turn brown and blemished if squeezed. Bananas are mostly imported from Central America.

BEETS are mild and sweet. To prevent the red from bleeding, boil them whole without cutting the tops off. Beets contain large amounts of potassium, iron, and folic acid. The leaves contain the antioxidant beta-carotene. Beets are red, yellow, or striped inside. They are best kept in a plastic bag in the fridge and keep for about 6 months at 40 °F/4 °C, but only 10 days at room temperature.

BELL PEPPER Green bell peppers are not ripe and thus have a more distinct flavor than yellow or red ones. They contain vitamin C and should preferably be eaten raw. Bell peppers are best kept unwashed in a plastic bag in the fridge, and they are prone to bruising, cold temperatures, and desiccation, and do not keep at room temperature. Red and yellow bell peppers keep for about a week and green ones a little longer. The skin should be taut and firm.

BLACKBERRIES contain some potassium and are rich in fiber. You should not pick them until they are fully ripe. They keep for one day at room temperature, but you can freeze them. The berries are delicate, so pick them straight into a plastic bag, remove the air, and freeze immediately. Blackberries grow wild in Europe and North America.

BLUEBERRIES are a rich source of antioxidants. If you pick them in the wild, remember to pick only the blue berries and not the black. If you buy them, try to find a batch with berries that are equal in size and not shrivelled. Blueberries keep for a couple of days in the refrigerator, but are suitable for freezing. Cultivated

American blueberries are a little larger than their European counterpart, but contain lower levels of antioxidants than the ones that are picked in the wild. Other differences are that American berries are not blue inside and do not stain your hands.

CARROTS. Carrots arrived in Europe from Central Asia in the 12th century, when they were bright red in color. Carrots contain beta-carotene, a precursor of vitamin A, which causes the bright color. Remove the green tops and keep in a plastic bag in the fridge or a cool space. The green tops must be removed since they cause leaching of nutrients and make the carrots go soft.

CHERRIES. Cherries are rich in vitamin C. Cherries also contain potassium and fiber and some research claims that they have certain anti-inflammatory properties. Look for plump, firm, and unblemished berries with taught, shiny skin and undamaged stalks. Cherries keep for a couple of days at room temperature. They must not be squashed and should not be packed tight in a plastic bag. They are best kept spread out on a flat dish.

CHILLIES. There are many different kinds of chilli, both fresh and dried. Most chillies are green when unripe and turn red, orange, or yellow when ripe. Chillies should be kept in a plastic bag in the fridge, but not below 45 °F/8 °C.

CITRUS FRUITS can be kept at room temperature or in the fridge. Thin-skinned varieties get juicier if left out in the kitchen while thicker skinned fruit is better kept in the fridge. They do not continue to ripen after harvesting, however. Citrus fruits have long been associated with Christmas and winter in the north, but are harvested all year in different parts of the world.

CLEMENTINES, SATSUMAS, and MANDARINS. Mandarin is sometimes used as a generic term for all types of small citrus fruit, but it is a subspecies. It is full of seeds and is less popular than clementines and satsumas. These are small citrus fruits that are easy to peel and almost always seed free. The satsuma, whose peel has a green tinge despite being harvested when it is ripe, is sometimes imported from Spain between October and January, or from Morocco.

CRANBERRIES originated in Russia, but most of the cranberries sold in shops are North American. Cranberries contain plenty of antioxidants and may help to relieve urinary infection and caries. Cranberries are in season between August and October. They acquire their sweetness after the first frost. If they are picked earlier in the year they need to be frozen before they are used. Cranberries contain benzoic acid, which is a natural preservative.

CUCUMBERS contain more water than any other fruit. They should be very firm. Soft or flexible cucumbers are beginning to go bad. Choose locally grown cucumbers rather than imported ones. Cucumbers keep best in a plastic bag in the fridge at 45–55 °F/ 7–14 °C. They go soft quickly if kept at room temperature and are sensitive to low temperatures. Do not remove the plastic wrapping as it protects against desiccation, bruising, and ethylene gas emitted by other vegetables that may cause them to ripen faster.

CURRANTS, RED and BLACK. Currants have been popular since the Middle Ages, but were not grown commercially until the end of the 19th century. Currants are red, black, yellow, or white. Regardless of color, they contain vitamin C and fiber. They keep for 2–3 days at room temperature and for about a week in the fridge. Currants freeze very well.

DATES are approximately 1½ inches/4 cm-long stone fruits rich in fiber and potassium, vitamin A, and vitamin D. Dates keep well and do not dry out. They keep for up to two months at about freezing point. They can be thawed and refrozen. Dates are imported all year from Israel and North Africa, where they are harvested between October and January.

FRESH HERBS. Smell the herbs when you are out shopping to determine which ones to buy. One tablespoon of fresh herbs equals about one teaspoon of dried herbs. If you buy them fresh in pots they will keep longer if they are watered regularly. Bunches of herbs are best kept in a plastic bag in the fridge. Just rinse as much as you are going to use or they will start rotting. Herbs keep for about a year in the freezer.

GRAPEFRUIT has an aromatic and fresh, but slightly bitter, taste that comes from the quinine it contains. One a day will provide the daily recommended intake of vitamin C. Choose a fruit that is firm and unblemished. How long it keeps depends on the country of origin, but it is best kept in a chiller cabinet at 50–75 °F/ 10–15 °C. People suffering from cardiovascular conditions should avoid eating grapefruit!

GRAPES are always harvested when they are ripe and do not keep well. They should be eaten straight away or stored in a plastic bag away from other fruit in the refrigerator, where they keep for up to a week. They taste best if they are left at room temperature 20 minutes before serving.

KIWIS can be eaten with or without the skin. Green kiwis are the most common variety found in shops, but you can also buy yellow ones that are a little sweeter. The fruits ripen after a few days at room temperature and faster if you put them in a plastic bag. Unripe kiwis can be kept in a plastic bag in the fridge for up to three weeks. Throw away any wrinkled or crushed fruit. The kiwi is named for the New Zealand national bird. New Zealand is the world's largest exporter of kiwi fruit.

LIMES are related to lemons and are used in the same way, but they have a more rounded taste and are more aromatic. Limes prefer the warmer part of the fridge. You can buy them all year, but only from tropical countries since they are sensitive to frost.

LINGONBERRIES/COWBERRIES contain average amounts of calcium, iron, vitamin C, and vitamin E. They are harvested in the fall and keep for a couple of weeks or up to a month in a plastic container lined with kitchen paper in the fridge. Lingonberries contain benzoic acid, which is a natural preservative. The jam does not need cooking and keeps well with only a small amount of added sugar. Fresh berries can also be frozen.

MANGOS contain carotene and antioxidants. Apply light pressure on the fruit to determine if it is ripe. It should yield to pressure, but it must not be too soft. You can smell it too, but the color provides no information since there are over a thousand known types that vary in color. Mangos keep for up to two weeks in the fridge. At room temperature they ripen quickly in a bag together with an apple or a banana. Ripe mangos can be kept in the fridge for a few days, but not in temperatures below 50 °F/10 °C. Mangos are exported all year round from, for example, Israel, Mali, the USA, and South America.

MELONS are related to pumpkins and cucumber. There are many different species that belong either to the sweet melon or to the watermelon family. The seeds of sweet melons are clustered at the center of the fruit while watermelon seeds are lodged in the pulp (read more under watermelon). It is important to use your sense of smell when choosing a melon. If the base of the flower (at the opposite end of the stalk) is fragrant, the melon is ripe. Keep whole melons at room temperature. Cut melons should be kept in the fridge. Melons produce ethylene gas, which speeds up the ripening process.

NECTARINE is a kind of peach with smooth skin and often a more distinct taste than peaches. Unripe nectarines ripen at room temperature. Unripe fruit should be kept in the fridge in a plastic bag. At room temperature ripe fruit keeps for a couple of days. Nectarines produce a lot of ethylene gas and only keep for a short period.

ORANGES. All citrus fruits are rich in vitamin C and a sweet pressed orange is a tasty way of getting your daily dose. Avoid very large oranges as they are usually too bland. Look for smooth, thin-skinned oranges that are heavy for their size. They are best kept in the fridge, but may keep for up to one to two weeks at room temperature. Remember that if you store your oranges in a cold place, the juice you get out of them will be cold. Oranges are cultivated in many parts of the world, but the main producers are Brazil and the USA. You can only buy Mediterranean oranges during the winter.

PAPAYAS contain vitamins A and C and are eaten in the same ways as melons. They keep best in the fridge. At 50 °F/10 °C they keep for up to three weeks. Unripe fruit ripens in a couple of days at room temperature. The greenish yellow skin is inedible and the orange flesh is sweet and aromatic. The ripe fruit should be uniform in color. Press a little lime juice over the papaya to bring out the flavor. The seeds are not normally eaten, although they are edible. They are peppery and taste a little like cress—not suitable for juices or smoothies.

PASSION FRUIT. There are several types of passion fruit including the purple granadilla normally found in shops. All contain potassium and beta-carotene. A passion fruit should be firm and a little, but not too, wrinkled. Make sure it is not too light-weight; that may be a sign that it has dried out inside. Passion fruit keeps for 3–4 weeks at 45–50 °F/7–10 °C.

PEACHES contain vitamins A, B, and C. They ripen quickly at room temperature and can only be left out for a couple of days at the most. They keep for up to two weeks at freezing point. Keep them in a plastic bag to prevent desiccation. Peaches are exported from southern Europe between May and September and December and January.

PEARS have been cultivated for thousands of years. They contain potassium, riboflavin (vitamin B2), and vitamins A and C. Pears do not keep well and are best stored in a plastic bag in the fridge. Take them out of the fridge and leave at room temperature for a few days to allow them to develop their flavor before

eating. Pears produce ethylene gas, which causes other fruits nearby to ripen faster.

PHYSALIS / CAPE GOOSEBERRY. The fruits are enclosed in a brown, papery, inedible husk. The whole of the fruit, including the skin, is edible. The physalis / cape gooseberry belongs to the same family as potatoes and contains plenty of vitamins A and C. Store for up to a couple of weeks in the fridge without removing the husk, or freeze.

PINEAPPLES are in fact a pseudocarp, or false, fruit, made up of many small berries that are joined together. They are an excellent source of vitamin C. The tangy taste makes them ideal for making juices and smoothies. Check that the pineapple is ripe by pulling out one of the leaves at the bottom. If it comes out easily, the fruit is ripe. There is, however, a risk that it is overripe, so it is always better to buy one that is unripe and leave it to ripen at home in the fridge, where it keeps for up to a week. It keeps for about three days at room temperature. Pineapples are cultivated in most of the tropical parts of the world and are usually exported from Central America and the Ivory Coast.

PLUMS are stone fruits that come in many colors and sizes. Unripe fruit ripens at room temperature in about a day, while ripe plums are best kept cool in the fridge.

POMEGRANATES. The edible part of a pomegranate is the seeds that are embedded in a jelly-like substance. The seeds contain a bright pigment that gives the color to grenadine, which is used in various cocktails. Pomegranates contain exceptionally high levels of antioxidants and may contribute to lowering blood pressure. They are mainly available during the winter. Ripe pomegranates are dark red, but it is better to choose an unripe fruit since they do not keep for more than about two weeks in the refrigerator.

RASPBERRIES. European raspberries are nearly always red, while black raspberries are common in the United States. Raspberries contain manganese, vitamin C, and fiber. The berries should be of an even color and do not keep for more than two days at the most.

RHUBARB. Rhubarb quickly goes limp at room temperature, but will keep in the refrigerator for a week wrapped in plastic wrap. Rhubarb contains oxalic acid, which should be boiled off before the rhubarb is served to small children or people who suffer from kidney stones. Never consume large quantities of oxalic acid.

SHARON FRUITS look like tomatoes, but should be eaten while they are still firm. The flesh of ripe sharon fruits is almost transparent and the skin almost as thin as that of a tomato. Store at freezing point, but keep the fruit at room temperature for a couple of hours before eating. Unripe fruit ripens in a couple of days at room temperature.

STRAWBERRIES contain more vitamin C than do oranges. Choose fruit that is not overripe or crushed. Strawberries turn bad quickly if they are crushed together in a box. They will keep in the refrigerator for a short period and are at their absolute best during the first 24 hours after picking. Remove the stalks and freeze the berries, either whole or sliced with a little added sugar. Strawberries are primarily cultivated in the USA, Poland, Japan, Italy, Spain, and Belgium.

TOMATOES. Tomatoes belong to the same family as bell peppers, potatoes, and tobacco. Unripe tomatoes should be stored at room temperature. After that the fridge is the best place for them, but take them out before serving; it improves the flavor. Tomatoes should not be kept together with apples since that speeds up the ripening process. Green, unripe tomatoes contain solanine and should not be eaten.

WATERMELON. The most common type of watermelon is green, but speckled or yellow-skinned watermelons exist too. They contain small amounts of vitamins A and B. They work well in smoothies because of the high water content. Choose a firm melon and make sure that it does not sound hollow when you tap it. Watermelons can be kept for up to 12 days at room temperature depending on type and on how ripe they are. Ideal storage conditions are a temperature of 10–50 ºF/5–9 ºC and a humid atmosphere.

MORE INGREDIENTS

Frozen Fruits and Berries

Deep frozen fruits and berries are becoming increasingly common. These days, you can buy most fruits and vegetables from the frozen food department all year; you can even buy mixed fruits ready for the blender. These are excellent substitutes for fresh fruit if they have been frozen immediately after harvesting.

It is a good idea to freeze your own fruit and vegetables in season. You will always have a ready supply for making smoothies and you will know exactly what is in your bags. Moreover, fruit is cheaper and better in season. Instructions for how to freeze fruit can be found on pages 12–13.

Dried Fruits and Berries

Many fruits and berries sold in shops are dried. This is an excellent alternative when it is hard to find fresh fruit. Make sure they are all natural and that they contain no added sugar, oil, flavorings, colorings or preservatives. Organically grown fruits without any trace of pesticides are to be preferred. The best produce lists no ingredients on the label other than the fruit. If you are making your smoothies with dried berries or fruit you should soak them before use—the larger the fruits or berries, the longer you need to soak them. Never pour hot or, worse, scalding water over the fruit since it will destroy nutrients. I always recommend that you wash dried fruit before you soak it unless the label states that it has been washed before drying.

Preserved Fruits and Berries

I prefer not to use preserved fruit in my smoothies, but if you do, remember to use fruit that is not preserved in syrup or contains coloring, flavoring, or other additives. It is best is if it has been preserved in its own juice.

Berry Powders and Super Berries

If you are unable to get hold of nutritious berries fresh, you can buy powders that you mix into your smoothie. Powders are made from freeze-dried whole berries, including skin and seeds. They are dried gently at 85 °F/ 30 °C to preserve vitamins, flavonoids, and minerals. Açaí berries, blueberries, pomegranates, raspberries, strawberries, rosehips, and cranberries can be purchased in powdered form. Powdered berries keep for up to 18 months, which is very useful. When you are adding fruit powders to a smoothie, remember that the flavors are highly concentrated.

AÇAI is considered to be the most nutritious super berry of them all. American studies have shown that they can destroy leukaemia cells, and they are famous for high vitamin and antioxidant content.

GOJI has been called a super berry because of the beneficial effect it has on the immune system. In China it is claimed to prolong life, and the berries have been used in Chinese medicine for thousands of years.

INKA is related to physalis and is considered to be the most nutritious berry in the world. It is extremely protein rich and has a beneficial effect on cholesterol levels. Other super berries are mulberries and barberries.

The best thing about these healthy, dried berries—apart from the fact that you can buy them all year round and that they keep forever—is that they are extremely tasty. Super berries are sold dried or in the form of juice.

Base Liquids

You can make a smoothie with almost anything you like; use your imagination and experiment to find your favorites.

Dairy products: milk, buttermilk, yogurt, quark, crème fraîche, cream, Greek yogurt, and feta cheese are all suitable. Just keep in mind that some of these ingredients are rather fatty and calorie rich, and should therefore not be consumed on a daily basis. Ice cream, frozen yogurt, sorbet, frozen fruit juices, frozen fruit, and frozen berries can all be used to make iced smoothies.

If you are lactose intolerant or just prefer to avoid dairy products, you can replace them with a lactose-free alternative such as soy yogurt, soy ice cream, oat milk, nut milk, silken tofu, etc. There are a lot to choose from in the shops, but some of these ingredients can easily be made at home. Oat milk and milk made from nuts and seeds are easy to make. Why not try them instead of dairy products next time you make a smoothie?

OAT MILK is made from porridge oats. Vegans should note that vitamin D from sheep's wool is used in some brands.

SOY MILK is made from soy beans, but you can make it at home from soy flour. It is the most protein rich of all plant milks. You can also buy soy ice cream or soy yogurt for your smoothie.

RICE MILK is made from brown rice. It is lactose, cholesterol, and sugar free and has a low fat content, but it contains more carbohydrates than cow's milk.

NUT MILK is made from soaked and blended beans or nuts such as cashews, hazelnuts, or walnuts.

COCONUT MILK comes from coconuts, which are a seed and not a nut. Some people are allergic to coconuts, but that is rare.

Fibers

The body cannot process plant fibers, but they are good for us since they slow down digestion. Vegetables, fruits, and wholemeal grain contain a lot of fiber.

Extra fiber can be provided by oat bran, wheat bran and ground linseeds. These help to balance bodily functions and are all excellent breakfast alternatives. Fibers help keep up energy levels during the day and give you a feeling of satisfaction after a meal.

Nutritious Flavor Enhancers

CARDAMOM contains plenty of antioxidants; it has a calming effect and aids digestion. Cardamom and ginger taken in the morning is said to cure a hangover.

CINNAMON is the bark of a tree that grows in Sri Lanka. Some scientists claim it has beneficial health effects. Cinnamon is used to flavor stews, soups, and desserts, but above all for sprinkling on yogurt and other dairy products.

COCOA POWDER has been much praised in the past few years, and chocolate bars have almost been given health food status. Cocoa has a beneficial effect on blood pressure and is rich in antioxidants.

GINGER is said to have many healing properties. It has long been used in Chinese medicine. It can relieve articular problems, headache, and stomach pain as well stimulate metabolism. But more than anything—it is delicious!

LICORICE is naturally sweet, which means that no sugar needs to be added. Eating too much licorice, however, may have negative effects on muscles and blood pressure.

Algae

Algae are an excellent protein source. We can absorb four times as much protein from the blue-green spirulina alga than from meat. Spirulina has been called "the alga that could put a stop to world famine." It is so nutritious that NASA give it to their astronauts in space. Other highly nutritious algae include chlorella, arame, wakame, and dulse.

Nuts and Seeds

ALMONDS are energy rich and contain muscle-building nutrients. They contain some monounsaturated fat and a lot of protein and vitamin E. Almond butter is sold in health food shops and can be used in smoothies.

BRAZIL NUTS are a rich source of protein, selenium, and zinc. Of the nut 70% is fat, most of which is omega 6; some of the fat is omega 3. Brazil nuts should be white inside; if they are yellow they are turning rancid.

HAZELNUTS contain large amounts of vitamin E, protein, and fat. Like all nuts they should be consumed in moderation.

HEMP SEEDS come from the same herb as cannabis, but the seed is entirely free of illegal substances. The hemp seed—which is really a nut—is the fruit of this herb. Soy beans are the only food that contains more protein than hemp seeds. They also contain large amounts of polyunsaturated fatty acids.

LINSEED is extremely nutritious and contains, for example, iron, phosphorus, potassium, calcium, zinc, and magnesium. Linseed is sold whole or crushed, and aids digestion. Like psyllium husks, it forms a mucilaginous layer in the gut, which aids peristalsis. Some sources recommend limiting your intake of crushed linseed to about two tablespoons per day.

PECAN NUTS are the pits of a kind of hickory fruit. They contain 72% fat, 63% of which is polyunsaturated. They also contain large amounts of antioxidants, especially in the brown outer skin of the pit.

PINE NUTS contain a lot of zinc, iron, protein, and polyunsaturated fats.

PISTACHIOS are not nuts but seeds, so they are quite safe for those allergic to nuts to eat. Red pistachios are artificially colored, so you should go for the plain variety. Pistachios contain a lot of fat and protein.

PUMPKIN SEEDS contain zinc and many types of antioxidant, high levels of protein, and a lot of polyunsaturated fat. It makes a nutritious snack, with anti-inflammatory properties. Toast or use in salads.

SESAME SEEDS are made up of 50% fats, nearly all of which are beneficial. They have a protein content of 18%. Ground sesame seeds are very useful in smoothies.

SUNFLOWER SEEDS are found at the center of the sunflower. They are rich in vitamin E, omega 6, and monounsaturated fatty acids as well as in vitamin B5, which relieves stress symptoms.

WALNUTS are very nutritious, especially for vegetarians, since they contain large amounts of omega 3 fatty acid.

Protein Powders

Examples of protein-rich powders or products are raw rice protein, tempeh, miso, powdered egg white, ground nuts, soy milk, and algae. Spirulina contains as much as 65% protein. Ask at your health food shop.

Cold-pressed Oils

Enrich your smoothies by adding nutritious cold-pressed coconut, linseed, or hempseed oil. Ask at your health food shop.

FRUIT & BERRY SMOOTHIES

NECTARINE & RASPBERRY

2 glasses

3 nectarines

2 cups/200 g raspberries

2 apples

honey or corn syrup

Wash all the fruit and berries. Peel, quarter, and core the apples and pass through a juicer. Cut the nectarines in half and remove the pits. Blend the nectarines, raspberries, and water until smooth. Add honey or corn syrup to taste.

Serve with raspberries on skewers.

TIP: Use honeydew melon instead of nectarines for a sweeter, milder version. If you are in a hurry, use a good-quality commercial apple juice instead of apples.

Acacia honey comes from the nectar of the *Robinia pseudoacacia*, which means "false acacia."
Because of the high fruit sugar content, acacia honey is liquid rather than set.

BLACKCURRANT & RASPBERRY

2 glasses

generous 2 cups/250 g blackcurrants

generous 2 cups/250 g raspberries

2 apples

Wash the apples and rinse the berries. Peel, quarter, and core the apples. Blend until smooth.

Serve with plenty of berries on top.

TIP: For a more liquid smoothie, juice the apples first or pass them through a fine-meshed sieve.

Both raspberries and blackcurrants contain large amounts of vitamin C. You can freeze the berries after harvesting and use them out of season.

WATERMELON, RASPBERRY, & MINT

2 glasses

¼ medium-size watermelon

generous 2 cups/250 g raspberries

5 mint leaves

Wash the fruit and berries. Cut the watermelon in half, remove the seeds, scoop out the pulp, and place it in a blender. Add raspberries and mint. Blend until smooth.

Serve with watermelon slices and raspberries.

TIP: Juice the watermelon, raspberries, and mint for a smoother texture.

Watermelon pulp is rich in antioxidants, but the seeds contain even more. Do not spit them out—eat them too. Adding them to the smoothie is not recommended, however.

ORANGE & MANGO

2 glasses

4 oranges

1 mango

½ lime

Wash all the fruit. Press the oranges and the lime. Be sure to discard the seeds since they will add a bitter taste. Use a potato peeler to peel the mango. Dice—remember there is a large pit inside. Pour the fresh orange juice and mango into a blender and blend until smooth.

Serve with orange wedges.

TIP: Add a few strawberries to make this even more delicious.

Mango is not only used to make chutney, it is the new peach! Pick a good mango by smelling it and squeezing it gently. Mango contains beta-carotene, just like carrots. It is supposed to give you a quicker tan.

RASPBERRY & PASSION FRUIT

2 glasses

generous 2 cups/250 g raspberries

3 passion fruits

¼ cantaloupe melon

Wash all the fruits and berries. Cut the melon in half, remove the seeds and peel, and put the pulp in a blender. Cut the passion fruits in half, scoop out the pulp, and pass through a fine-meshed sieve. Blend all the ingredients until smooth.

TIP: Garnish with a frosted rim. Pour some superfine sugar on a plate, then run a lemon or lime wedge around the rim of the glass. Dip the glass into the sugar, or replace the sugar with grated chocolate, cocoa, cinnamon, or some other suitable herb or spice.

Raspberries are rich in fiber and good for the immune system.
Pick the fresh berries in season.

BLUEBERRY & CINNAMON

2 glasses

2 apples

generous 2 cups/250 g blueberries

1 pinch of cinnamon

7 tbsp/100 ml water

½ lime

honey

Peel, quarter, and core the apples
Place in a blender with the blueberries,
cinnamon, and water. Press the lime,
and be sure to discard the seeds since
they will add a bitter taste. Blend until
smooth. Add honey to taste.

TIP: For a more liquid smoothie, juice
the apples (including the peel) first and
omit the water.

Cinnamon is Italian for "little tubes." It is the bark of a tree that grows in Sri Lanka, and it was known by the ancient Egyptians as early as 1500 B.C. The Arabs told many tales to keep the price of cinnamon high. One of them involved some birds that roost on a top of a steep mountain where no one could reach, and who fed their young with cinnamon sticks. In order to get to the cinnamon, the Arabs fed the birds pieces of meat that were so large and heavy that the nests fell to the ground. No wonder that cinnamon was an expensive spice.

MANGO & PASSION FRUIT

2 glasses

2 large mangos

4 passion fruits

generous ¾ cup/200 ml ice water

passion fruit to garnish

Wash all the fruit. Put one passion fruit aside for garnish. Divide the passion fruits, scoop out the pulp, and sieve out the seeds (optional). Peel the mango and cut it into chunks—remember there is a large pit in the middle. Blend the passion fruit, mango, and water until smooth. Serve with passion fruit.

TIP: Get rid of the passion fruit seeds by pouring a little water into the fruit. Mix the water and pulp until separated. Pass through a fine mesh and use only the liquid.

Passion fruit is in fact a berry which is said to relieve asthma. It comes from a climbing plant that can become 50 feet/15 meters tall. The dark, purple skin of the fresh fruit is smooth. The name comes from the passion flower, which in appearance symbolizes the passion (suffering) of Christ. The yellow-skinned Maracuja is another member of the passion flower family.

ORANGE, MANGO, & POMEGRANATE

2 glasses

4 oranges

1 mango

1 pomegranate

Wash all the fruit. Press the oranges, and make sure you remove the seeds since they will add a bitter taste. Use a citrus press to extract the pomegranate juice. Peel the mango and dice. Do not forget there is a large pit inside. Blend the fresh orange–pomegranate juice and mango until smooth.

Top with a few pomegranate seeds.

TIP: To make a "sunrise" effect, blend orange and mango only. Transfer to a glass and pour pomegranate juice on top.

Separating the pomegranate seeds from the skin is easier if you first roll the pomegranate against a hard surface. Cut it in half and beat the halves with a wooden spoon to loosen the seeds.

PINEAPPLE & LEMON BALM

2 glasses

½ pineapple

6 lemon balm leaves

Wash the pineapple and lemon balm carefully. Cut the pineapple in half, remove the leaves, peel, and hard center. Dice. Blend the fruit and lemon balm until smooth.

Serve with pieces of pineapple on the side.

TIP: Pass everything through a juicer instead to make a less pulpy smoothie. Experiment by adding chilli or other spices.

Pineapple is an attractive plant that grows to about 3 feet/1 meter in height. When the purple flowers ripen they form berries that fuse together to form the pineapple. It has been said to be good for people suffering from cancer or from cardiovascular or intestinal disease. Allegedly, you will smell sweet if you eat a lot of pineapple. So, there are many good reasons for doing so, even though these claims have to be taken with a grain of salt.

AÇAI & STRAWBERRY

2 glasses

generous 3 cups/350 g strawberries

2 pears

4 tsp açaí powder

Wash the strawberries and pears.
Quarter, core, and juice the pears.
Destalk the strawberries. Blend the
juice, strawberries, and berry powder
until smooth.

TIP: Use a berry powder of your
choice to add flavor and goodness
to your smoothies.

In order for us to benefit from all the antioxidants, vitamins, and minerals present in açaí berries, they
must either be eaten fresh or frozen immediately after harvesting. Only 10% of the berry is edible,
the seed makes up the remaining 90%.

APRICOT & ORANGE

2 glasses

6 ripe apricots

3 oranges

½ lime

Wash the fruit. Press the orange and the lime, and make sure you discard the seeds since they will add a bitter taste. Divide the apricots and remove the pits. Blend all the ingredients until smooth.

TIP: Use dried apricots if you cannot find fresh ones. They need to be soaked for about an hour before using.

The Latin for apricot is *Prunus armeniaca*, which means "Armenian plum." It was long believed that apricots came from Armenia, but now we know they originated in China, where they were cultivated as far back as 4,000–5,000 years ago. Today, 85% of apricots are grown in a part of Turkey that was formerly part of Armenia. Eat them raw, cook them, or use them to make jam or liqueur.

GUAVA & BLUEBERRY

2 glasses

1 guava

2 cups/200 g blueberries

2 cups/200 g strawberries

1 passion fruit

honey

Wash the fruit and berries. Peel the guava and cut it in half. Remove the seeds and dice. Cut the passion fruit in half, scoop out the pulp, and pass it through a fine mesh. Destalk the strawberries. Blend all the ingredients until smooth. Sweeten with honey to taste.

TIP: The guava can be replaced with honeydew melon.

Guavas contain a lot of white, hard, edible seeds.
One guava can contain well over six hundred seeds.

MANGO & STRAWBERRY

2 glasses

1 mango

2 cups/200 g strawberries

generous ¾ cup/200 ml water

Wash the mango and strawberries carefully. Peel the mango and dice. Do not forget there is a large pit inside. Destalk the strawberries and blend all the ingredients until smooth.

TIP: You can replace the strawberries with raspberries.

Did you know that strawberries contain more vitamin C than oranges?
Five strawberries are all you need to get your daily allowance of vitamin C.

BANANA & PASSION FRUIT

2 glasses

3 bananas

4 passion fruits

10 green grapes

½ lime

generous ¾ cup/200 ml ice water

Wash the fruit. Peel the bananas, cut the passion fruits in half, scoop out the pulp, and sieve out the seeds. Discard the grape seeds, add the lime juice, and blend until smooth.

TIP: Note that no liquid can be extracted from bananas; put them straight into the blender. Bananas add sweetness and bulk to tart and watery smoothies, and can be used in many recipes.

There are some fifty different types of banana in the world. Two types of eating banana have been produced through cross-breeding—the sweet "dessert" banana and the more floury plantain, or "cooking" banana. Plantains are very common in South America, Africa, and India, where they are used for cooking in much the same ways as potatoes. Dessert bananas include the apple banana, which is small, yellow, and smells faintly of apples, and the rarer red banana.

MANGO & ROSEHIP

2 glasses

2 large mangos

10 rosehips or 2 tsp powdered rosehips

generous ¾ cup/200 ml ice water

Wash all the fruit. Peel the mango and dice. Remember there is a large pit inside. Split the rosehips, remove the seeds and stalks, then chop. Blend the rosehips and water until smooth, then add the mango and blend again until smooth.

Serve with mango on the side.

TIP: When rosehips are not in season, use powdered rosehips instead. It can be found in health food shops.

Any rosehips that are left on the bush will go black in the winter, but they can still be used for food.

BLACKBERRY, APPLE, & CINNAMON

2 glasses

3 apples or generous ¾ cup/200 ml apple juice

2 cups/200 g blackberries

1 cup/100 g raspberries

7 tbsp/100 ml water

1 pinch cinnamon

Wash all the fruit carefully. Destalk, core, and dice the apples and pass them through a juicer or use a good commercial brand instead. Blend all the ingredients until smooth.

TIP: Add 4 tablespoons of vanilla-flavored quark instead of water for a more substantial smoothie.

Blackberry is a generic name for a collection of hybrids comprising some thirty species.
Blackberries are notable for their high nutritional content of dietary fibers, vitamin C, vitamin K, and folic acid.

STRAWBERRY & CHILLI

2 glasses

generous 3 cups/350 g strawberries

1 lime

½ chilli (+2 for garnish)

7 tbsp/100 ml ice water

6 ice cubes

corn syrup

Wash the strawberries, lime, and chillies. Destalk the strawberries and make sure that no green or hard bits end up in the blender. Split the chilli, remove the seeds and white membranes, then chop the chilli. Blend all the ingredients until smooth. Add corn syrup to taste.

TIP: Replace the strawberries with two mangos for another delicious combination. Strawberries and mango go well with chilli. Instead, why not try adding a piece of lemon grass?

The strength of chilli is not in the seeds, but in the membranes and the base of the stalk. Water is no remedy against the burning sensation resulting from more than you like since the strength is in the capsaicin, an oil that is not water soluble. Drink a soothing glass of milk instead.

MANDARIN & MANGO

2 glasses

1 mango

4 mandarins

½ lime

generous ¾ cup/200 ml sparkling mineral water

Peel the mango and dice. Remember there is a large pit inside. Peel the mandarins and discard the white pith and the peel (or press out the juice). Press the lime and be sure to remove the seeds. Blend the ingredients until smooth. Pour over ice cubes and fill up with sparkling mineral water.

Serve with a straw and decorate with mandarin sections.

TIP: For a more traditional smoothie, blend all the ingredients except the sparkling water. Replace it with 7 tbsps/100 ml plain water and 7 tbsp/100 ml good-quality apple juice.

Mandarin is a generic name for mandarins, clementines, satsumas, and tangerines. The name probably derives from the yellow color associated with the traditional dress worn by Chinese officials, or mandarins.

GRAPEFRUIT & STRAWBERRY

2 glasses

3 blood grapefruits

generous 2 cups/250 g strawberries

generous ¾ cup/200 ml water

honey

Wash all the fruit and berries. Peel the grapefruits, discard the membranes and peel. Destalk the strawberries, add the rest of the ingredients, and blend until smooth.

TIP: If you do not like the bitterness of grapefruit, use oranges or any other citrus fruit instead.

Strawberries are a cross between two types of wild strawberry, and the resulting hybrid was then crossed with a third variety. This successful blend of wild strawberries was called *Fragaria ananassa*, which refers to their being "fragrant." Those allergic to ordinary strawberries can usually tolerate white strawberries, which lack the red pigment.

BLUEBERRY & MELON

2 glasses

½ honeydew melon

2 cups/200 g blueberries

1 cup/100 g raspberries

honey to taste

Wash all the fruit and berries. Cut the melon in half, remove the seeds, peel, and place the flesh in a blender with the rest of the ingredients. Blend until smooth.

Serve with whole blueberries.

TIP: Use cloudberries instead of blueberries and increase the amount of raspberries to 2 cups/200 g.

Melon is related to cucumber and is suitable for making smoothies because of the high water content. Choose one that feels heavy and smells sweet round the base of the stalk.

STRAWBERRY & BASIL

2 glasses

generous 3 cups/350 g strawberries

6 basil leaves

generous ¾ cup/200 ml water

corn syrup

4 ice cubes

Wash the strawberries and basil leaves. Destalk the strawberries. Blend all the ingredients until smooth.

Serve with basil leaves.

TIP: Replace the basil with other fresh herbs, e.g. lemon balm, mint, lemongrass, a little rosemary. Only use the soft leaves.

Basil is not only used in food, but in liqueurs, cough mixtures, and perfumes. It was a symbol of hate to the ancient Romans, but the meaning has changed over the years and in Italy today it symbolizes love. Young Italian women put it in their hair as a sign that they are looking for love, and it is said to attract men by the sweet smell.

RASPBERRY & PEAR

2 glasses

3 ripe pears
generous 2 cups/250 g raspberries
generous ¾ cup/200 ml ice water
honey

Wash the pears and raspberries. Peel, quarter, and core the pears. Place in a blender, add raspberries and water. Blend until smooth. Add honey to taste.

Serve with raspberries.

TIP: For a more liquid smoothie, juice the pears and add only 7 tablespoons/100 ml of water. Vary with a few pieces of mango.

Pears contain twice as much fiber as apples, but they keep less well. Buy unripe pears and keep them in the fridge. Store the pears together with apples, which emit a gas that causes the pears to ripen faster.

MANGO & CHILLI

2 glasses

2 large mangos

¼ red chilli

generous ¾ cup/200 ml ice water

Peel the mango and dice. Remember it has a large pit. Add the water and chopped chilli—membranes and seeds removed. Blend until smooth.

Serve with chillies.

TIP: Add less chilli if you do not like it strong, but do try a little. Even a small amount enhances the flavor. Just add more if you like it.

Chilli stimulates metabolism. The strength of different chillies varies, so be careful. Among the most common are jalapeño, habanero, tabasco, and canario. You can buy dried chillies that work almost just as well as fresh, but be careful since the seeds are often included.

POMEGRANATE & GRAPEFRUIT

2 glasses

2 pomegranates

2 blood grapefruits

2 oranges

4 ice cubes

Wash all the fruit (including the citrus peel to get rid of pesticide residues). Cut the pomegranates in half and extract the juice. Peel the grapefruits and discard the membranes, pith, and peel. Press the oranges. Blend until smooth.

Serve on the rocks and dilute it with a little water if it is too intense.

TIP: Just press the grapefruits if you do not want to remove the pith and membranes.

One grapefruit contains more than the daily recommended intake of vitamin C for adults. Pink or red grapefruits are sweeter than the standard yellow. Grapefruits do not grow in the wild. They were discovered in the 18th century in a West-Indian citrus plantation.

BLUEBERRY & PEAR

2 glasses

2 pears

½ lemon

2 cups/200 g blueberries

generous ¾ cup/200 ml water

honey

Peel, quarter, and core the pears. Press the lemon and make sure no seeds end up in the smoothie. Blend all the ingredients until smooth.

Serve with fresh blueberries.

Blueberries are extremely nutritious. They contain antioxidants such as ascorbic acid and lutein.
Blueberry tea has been used as a natural remedy to relieve stomach pains and improve eyesight and memory.
Use frozen blueberries if you cannot find fresh ones.

RED CURRANT & MANGO

2 glasses

2 cups/200 g red currants

1 cup/100 g strawberries

1 mango

1 apple

Rinse the berries and fruit. Destalk the strawberries and the currants. Dice the apple and pass through a masticating or centrifugal juicer. Peel the mango and dice. Remember there is a large pit inside. Blend all the ingredients until smooth.

TIP: Use good-quality commercial apple juice with no additives if you do not have time to make your own.

Wild and cultivated currants can be used for making wine.

ORANGE & BANANA

2 glasses

2 bananas

4 oranges

½ lemon

Wash all the fruit. Peel the bananas and place in the blender. Press the oranges and lemon, making sure you do not include any seeds—they will add a bitter taste. Blend until smooth.

Serve with lemon balm.

TIP: Add a few strawberries or raspberries for extra color and taste.

Oranges originally came from China. These days they are cultivated all over the world. Make a medicinal orange soup against the common cold by steeping 1 tablespoon chopped ginger, 2 tablespoons honey, and a handful of raisins in 2 cups/500 ml water. Refrigerate overnight and blend with the juice of one orange and two lemons.

RASPBERRY & BLUEBERRY

2 glasses

½ banana

generous 2 cups/250 g raspberries

2 cups/200 g blueberries

generous ¾ cup/200 ml ice water

honey or fructose

Wash all the fruit and berries carefully. Peel the banana. Blend until smooth.

Serve with fresh berries.

TIP: Use yogurt instead of water for a classic blueberry and raspberry smoothie.

Raspberries are clusters of many small, individual berries that each contain a seed.

KIWI & BANANA

2 glasses

2 oranges

2 kiwis

1 banana

7 tbsp/100 ml water

Wash all the fruit. Press the oranges. Peel and chop the kiwi, peel the bananas, and blend all the ingredients until smooth.

TIP: Dilute with water if the smoothie becomes too thick.

The mini bananas sold in shops seem to have no other purpose than to be attractive to young children. They look nice, but are no different from regular bananas.

MANGO & GINGER

2 glasses

2 mangos

1 inch/3 cm fresh ginger

3 apples or generous ¾ cup/200 ml apple juice

Wash all the fruit. Dice the apples and juice. Peel the mango and dice; remember the large pit inside. Grate the ginger (including the peel) using a fine grater. Blend all the ingredients until smooth.

TIP: Add a little water if the smoothie is turning too thick. Add some chilli powder or fresh chilli for extra bite. If you are buying your apple juice readymade, do not forget that it should be of good quality, freshly made, and additive free.

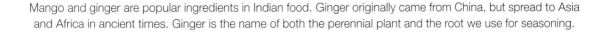

Mango and ginger are popular ingredients in Indian food. Ginger originally came from China, but spread to Asia and Africa in ancient times. Ginger is the name of both the perennial plant and the root we use for seasoning.

STRAWBERRY & PINEAPPLE

2 glasses

2 cups/200 g strawberries

½ pineapple

generous ¾ cup/200 ml ice water

½ lime

Wash all the fruit carefully. Destalk the strawberries. Cut the pineapple in half. Remove the leaves, peel, and the hard core. Place the pineapple, strawberries, and water in the blender. Cut the lime in half and squeeze out the juice, making sure you discard the seeds—they add a bitter taste. Blend until thick and smooth.

TIP: Try another version by juicing pineapples and strawberries. Leave out the water and pass the ingredients through a juicer instead.

Pineapples are sweet and excellent in desserts. If you are using pineapple in desserts that include cream and gelatine, add it as close to serving as possible since it contains bromeline, a substance which prevents gelatine from setting.

KIWI & MANGO

2 glasses

2 oranges

3 kiwis

1 mango

7 tbsp/100 ml ice water

Wash all the fruit. Press the oranges. Peel and chop the kiwi. Peel the mango and dice; remember there is a large pit inside. Blend until smooth.

TIP: When mangos are in season you can freeze them in batches in plastic bags. It is cheaper and better to use frozen fruit out of season than eating unripe fruit that has been stored for a long time and treated with preservatives. Fresh is always best, but fruit that is frozen directly after harvesting is fine too.

Until the 1960s, kiwis were called "Chinese gooseberries." Kiwis are often imported from New Zealand, but are in season in the Mediterranean between November and April. Ripe kiwis yield to light pressure. Watch out for very soft ones—they tend to taste bad.

MANGO & LEMON BALM

2 glasses

2 mangos

6 lemon balm leaves

generous ¾ cup/200 ml water

Peel the mango and dice; remember there is a large pit inside. Chop the lemon balm and blend with the mango and water until smooth.

TIP: You can use lemon balm extract instead of the leaves.

Lemon balm is cultivated, but can be found in the wild too.

COCONUT & PINEAPPLE

2 glasses

½ pineapple

1 banana

7 tbsp/100 ml coconut milk

½ lime

honey

4 ice cubes

Wash all the fruit carefully. Cut the pineapple in half. Remove the leaves, peel, and coarse center. Cut the lime in half and squeeze out the juice. Avoid the seeds; they add a bitter taste. Peel the banana. Place the pineapple, banana, lime juice, coconut milk, and ice cubes in the blender. Mix until thick and smooth. Add honey to taste.

Serve with coconut and pineapple on the side.

TIP: Always buy unsweetened coconut milk without additives and with a short best before date.

One of the great holiday classics is the Piña Colada. It is made with rum, pineapple, and coconut.
Make it by mixing ¼ cup/60 ml light rum, 2 tbsp/30 ml coconut milk, and 6 tbsps/90 ml pineapple juice—
but a smoothie is the healthier choice!

RASPBERRY & MANGO

2 glasses

1 mango

generous 2 cups/250 g raspberries

generous ¾ cup/200 ml water

½ lime

honey to taste

Wash the mango and raspberries carefully. Peel the mango and dice; remember there is a large pit inside. Press the lime and make sure you discard the seeds; they add a bitter taste. Blend all the ingredients until smooth.

TIP: Add a small pinch of chilli powder or a little chopped chilli.

Raspberries are full of an unusual form of antioxidant that cannot be found in any other food.
Buy raspberries that are evenly colored and remember that they keep for only a couple of days.

BLACKCURRANT & GRAPEFRUIT

2 glasses

1 pear

1 grapefruit

2 cups/200 g blackcurrants

1 cup/100 g raspberries

7 tbsp/100 ml ice water

Wash all the fruit. Rinse the berries. Peel the pear, quarter it, and remove the core. Peel the grapefruit and discard the pith, membranes, and peel. Blend all the ingredients until smooth. Serve with blackcurrants on a cocktail stick

TIP: Add a few ice cubes instead of water for a more icy result.

Blackcurrants contain antioxidants that are said to be good for the eyesight. They are rich in vitamin C too, as well as in vitamins, fibers, and folic acid.

MELON & RASPBERRY

2 glasses

1 honeydew melon
generous 2 cups/250 g raspberries
½ lime
4 ice cubes

Wash the fruit and berries, and leave them to dry. Cut the melon in half, remove the seeds and peel, and add to the blender. Cut the lime in half and press the juice straight into the blender, making sure you discard the seeds—they add a bitter taste. Add the raspberries and ice cubes and mix until thick and smooth.

Serve with raspberries or slices of melon on the side.

TIP: Add 1 banana for a thicker result.

Up to two hundred bananas can grow on one plant.
Bananas are not only a fruit; they are a herb and a berry too!

POMEGRANATE & WATERMELON

2 glasses

½ lime

2 pomegranates

¼ watermelon

4 ice cubes

Wash the fruit, including the melon. Press the lime. Cut the pomegranates in half and extract the juice. Cut the watermelon in half, remove seeds and peel, chop the flesh, and place it in the blender with the ice cubes. Blend until smooth.

TIP: The watermelon can be replaced with honeydew or Galia melon.

Watermelons are not related to other melons, and you cannot find a ripe one by using your sense of smell as you do with other melons. There is a certain amount of risk-taking involved when you purchase one. Choose one that does not make a hollow sound when you tap it.

CHERRY & BLUEBERRY

2 glasses

2 apples

2 cups/200 g cherries

1 banana

2 cups/200 g blueberries

Wash all the fruit and berries. Remove the stalks from the apples, then dice the apples and extract the juice. Remove the pits from the cherries and peel the banana. Blend all the ingredients until smooth.

TIP: If you are in a hurry or do not have access to a juicer, you can use a good-quality, additive-free commercial brand of apple juice instead.

The best apples are the ones you pick yourself or the local varieties that are available in the shops for a short period in the fall. Shops sometimes prefer imported brands from New Zealand or Argentina. Talk to your local shop and ask them to stock local varieties in season in order to create a demand.

MANDARIN & PAPAYA

2 glasses

6 mandarins, satsumas, or clementines

1 small papaya (ca. 10 oz/300 g)

½ lemon

Wash all the fruit. Press the mandarins and lemon, making sure that no seeds are included; they add a bitter taste. Cut the papaya in half, peel it, discard the seeds, then dice. Blend all the ingredients until smooth.

TIP: Add a little water if you find the taste too intense.

Mandarin is the generic name for clementines, satsumas, and tangerines. Mandarins contain a lot of seeds and are therefore often replaced by seedless clementines or satsumas. The clementine is a cross between a mandarin and a Seville orange. The smaller, more smooth-skinned satsuma is a Japanese variety. Tangerines look somewhat like a reddish orange.

WATERMELON, STRAWBERRY, & LIME

2 glasses

10 strawberries

¼ medium-size watermelon

1 lime

crushed ice

Destalk the strawberries. Cut the watermelon in half, remove the seeds, and place the flesh in a blender. Add the lime juice and strawberries, and blend until smooth. You can also juice the watermelon and strawberries if you do not like the taste of the pulp.

Serve with watermelon slices on the side.

TIP: Blend with plenty of ice on a hot summer day to make it more like a sorbet, and serve with strawberries. Do not forget to place a spoon or a thick straw in the glass.

Watermelons contain 90% water and make a refreshing juice.

PRUNE & ALMOND

2 glasses

3 apples

12 prunes, pitted

12 almonds

generous ¾ cup/200 ml water

Wash the apples and quarter, core, dice, and juice them. Blend the prunes, almonds, apple juice, and water until smooth.

Serve with prunes on the side.

TIP: If you are pressed for time, use a good commercial brand of apple juice, preferably organic and additive free.

Prunes are excellent as a mid-afternoon snack, or use them in porridge.
There are many other great dishes to make with prunes; they are even used for making wine.

MANGO & PINEAPPLE

2 glasses

1 mango

½ pineapple

½ lime

generous ¾ cup/200 ml water

Peel the mango and dice; remember there is a large pit inside. Cut the pineapple in half, remove the leaves, peel and remove the tough center. Press the lime, making sure you discard the seeds—they add a bitter taste. Blend all the ingredients until smooth.

Serve with mango slices on a cocktail stick.

TIP: Put the fruit through a juicer if you do not like the taste of the pulp. Dilute with a little water if the taste is too intense.

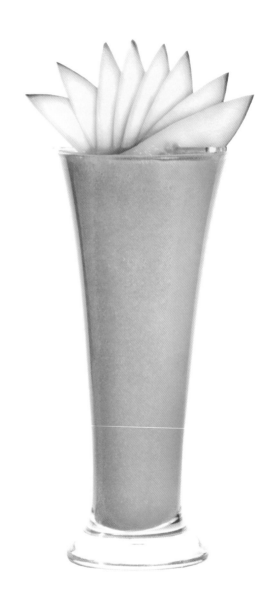

Limes are full of vitamin C. They are a popular cocktail ingredient and perfect for making smoothies. There are three types: the large, acidic, seedless one; a smaller, more aromatic one; and then the "real" lime, which is sweeter and resembles a clementine.

KIWI & ORANGE

2 glasses

½ banana

5 kiwis

2 oranges

1 grapefruit

7 tbsp/100 ml water

Wash all the fruit. Peel the banana. Peel and chop the kiwi. Press the oranges and grapefruit and make sure you discard the seeds; they add a bitter taste. Blend all the ingredients until smooth.

TIP: Do not blend the kiwi for too long in order to prevent the seeds from breaking.

You can wash and eat the kiwi peel. It is soft and full of flavor, and you will not notice the hairs—it is good for you. Kiwis have a high vitamin C and E content. It does not blend well with dairy products, however. Mix it with other berries and tropical fruits.

STRAWBERRY & BANANA

2 glasses

2 oranges

2 bananas

generous 2 cups/250 g strawberries

7 tbsp/100 ml water

Wash all the fruit. Press the oranges and peel the bananas. Blend all the ingredients until smooth.

TIP: Replace the strawberries with other tangy berries such as raspberries.

Most people know that oranges are full of vitamin C, but they contain many other nutrients that you will not get from an effervescent tablet. This orange berry contains plant substances and flavonoids. An orange a day gives a boost to your immune system and may lower blood pressure.

MELON & PASSION FRUIT

2 glasses

½ honeydew melon

¼ watermelon

6 passion fruits

½ lime

Wash all the fruit carefully. Remove the melon seeds, scoop out the flesh, and place in a blender. Press the lime and add the juice to the blender. Pass the passion fruit through a sieve before adding it. Blend all the ingredients until smooth.

Serve with passion fruit or melon slices.

TIP: Use a juicer instead if you prefer.

Both the watermelon and the honeydew melon are members of the gourd or *cucurbitaceae* family, but they are not related—they belong to different species.

NECTARINE & MANGO

2 glasses

2 nectarines

1 mango

2 oranges

½ lime

Wash the fruit. Press the oranges and lime and make sure you discard the seeds; they add a bitter taste. Remove the pits from the nectarines and dice. Peel the mango and dice; remember there is a large pit inside. Blend all the ingredients until smooth.

TIP: Vary with 1 cup/100 g fresh or frozen and thawed lingonberries (cowberries) or cranberries instead of nectarines.

Nectarines are peaches minus the downy peel. Nectarines and peaches may grow on the same tree, and there is really no reason for them to be sold separately. Peaches have been cultivated in China for over 4,000 years, but it was long believed they originated in Persia, thus the name. The name nectarine comes from "nectar"—the drink of the gods.

MELON & BANANA

2 glasses

1 honeydew melon

2 bananas

7 tbsp/100 ml freshly pressed apple juice

1 lime

Peel the bananas and place in the blender. Cut the melon in half, remove the seeds and peel, and place the flesh in the blender. Add lime juice, making sure you discard the pips; they add a bitter flavor. Add the freshly made apple juice. Blend all the ingredients until thick and smooth.

Serve with slices of melon.

TIP: Try other types of melon such as watermelon, Galia, or cantaloupe.

Bananas are best kept in a separate bowl.
Many other fruits emit ethylene gas, which causes them to ripen faster.

PAPAYA & MANDARIN

2 glasses

1 small papaya (ca. 10 oz/300 g)

6 mandarins

½ lime

4 ice cubes

Wash all the fruit. Press the lime and mandarins, making sure you discard the seeds—they add a bitter taste. Cut the papaya in half and remove the seeds. Scoop out the flesh, and chop and place in a blender with fresh lime juice, mandarin juice, and ice cubes. Blend all the ingredients until smooth.

Serve with papaya slices.

TIP: Papaya seeds are pretty, so sprinkle some on the smoothie to decorate. They are not bad for you but they do not taste that great either ...

Papaya is a tall plant that contains papain, a substance used to make drugs for digestive problems. Some say it may help you to lose weight.

RHUBARB & STRAWBERRY

2 glasses

2 apples

2 rhubarb stalks

2 cups/200 g strawberries

2–3 tsp honey or vanilla-flavored powdered sugar

Wash the fruit and berries. Dice the apples and pass through a centrifugal or masticating juicer. Peel and chop the rhubarb, discard the leaves and roots. Simmer the rhubarb and fresh apple juice on low heat for 5–6 minutes until the rhubarb has turned soft. Cool and blend with the strawberries and honey until smooth.

TIP: Add ¾ cup/150 g vanilla-flavored quark or vanilla yogurt for a milder version.

Rhubarb leaves contain oxalic acid, which is toxic. There is little risk of consuming it by eating the stalk, but you should use the young plants in early summer to avoid it. The oxalic acid disappears with cooking, but do not use an aluminum cooking vessel since oxalic acid reacts with aluminum. Pick or buy rhubarb in the summer and freeze for a ready supply all year.

PEACH & RASPBERRY

2 glasses

2 oranges

4 ripe peaches

2 cups/200 g raspberries

2 tbsp vanilla-flavored quark

Wash the fruit and berries. Press the oranges. Halve and core the peaches and dice. Place all the ingredients in a blender and blend until smooth. Pass through a fine mesh for an even smoother texture.

Serve with peach slices on the side.

TIP: Use nectarines if peaches are not available.

The skin of peaches is furry and they can grow on the same tree as nectarines. Always buy ripe peaches—they do not ripen after harvesting, and they do not keep for more than a couple of days.

MELON & GOJI BERRIES

2 glasses

1 honeydew melon

4 tsp dried goji berries

4 tsp dried cranberries

1 lime

Soak the goji berries and cranberries for an hour before use. Blend them with water until smooth. Wash the melon and cut it in half, remove the seeds and peel. Add the flesh to the blender. Cut the lime in half and add the juice to the other ingredients. Make sure you discard the seeds; they add a bitter taste. Blend until smooth.

TIP: Vary with watermelon.

One single goji berry contains more vitamin C than two oranges. Just imagine what a couple of goji berries can do for your smoothie! They also contain vital amino acids, iron, calcium, selenium, and zinc.

APPLE, PINEAPPLE & GINGER

2 glasses

½ pineapple

5 apples

1 inch/2–3 cm ginger

Cut the pineapple in half, remove the leaves, peel, and remove the tough center. Dice. Halve the apples, remove the stalks, and dice. Slice the ginger and put the slices and apples into a juicer. Transfer the juice to a blender, add pineapple chunks, and blend until thick and smooth. Serve on ice with ginger and green herbs for garnish.

TIP: Pass all the ingredients through the juicer for a more liquid smoothie.

Most people know that cucumber is 99% water, and that watermelons are 90% water surprises no one, but did you know that apples are 85% water? This does not mean they do not contain masses of nutrients and fiber, quite the reverse!

BLACKCURRANT & STRAWBERRY

2 glasses

generous 2 cups/250 g blackcurrants

2 cups/200 g strawberries

generous ¾ cup/200 ml fresh apple juice

1 tsp vanilla-flavor powdered sugar

ice cubes

Wash all the berries. Blend all the ingredients until thick and smooth.

Serve with a few blackcurrants.

TIP: Mix in 1 tbsp bran for some natural fiber. You cannot taste or feel the bran in a smoothie.

Vanilla tastes nice, but this spice arrived in Europe for a completely different reason. It was considered to be an aphrodisiac, which of course made it very popular in Europe in the 18th century. Men went so far as to flavor their pipe tobacco with vanilla seeds.

PLUM & ROSEHIP

2 glasses

6 yellow plums

2 tbsp rosehip powder

½ banana

2 apples

1 passion fruit

½ lemon

Wash all the fruit, including the banana. Cut the apples in half, remove the stalks, dice, and pass through a juicer. Remove the pits from the plums and chop. Cut the passion fruit in half, scoop out the flesh, and pass through a sieve to remove the seeds. Peel the bananas and slice. Press the lime. Blend everything until thick and smooth.

TIP: Try goji berries instead of rosehip powder. Any color plum will do.

Rosehips are rich in vitamins C and A.
Rosehips are not a fruit, but the base of the flower. The fruit itself is really a nut.

PEAR & PASSION FRUIT

2 glasses

4 pears

2 apples

½ banana

3 passion fruits

½ lime

Wash all the fruit. Cut the apples in half and quarter the pears, remove the stalks, and dice. Peel the lime and dice. Cut the passion fruits in half and scoop out the flesh. Alternate apples, pears, lime, and passion fruit in the juicer. Pour the juice into the blender, add banana, and blend until smooth. Serve on ice with a passion fruit wedge and a herb leaf on the side.

TIP: Scoop out a half passion fruit and sprinkle over the smoothie for an attractive effect.

Passion fruit is a berry. You can grow them yourself. Buy a passion fruit, separate the seeds from the flesh, and plant them in a pot. After a few months you will have a green seedling, which will in time grow to a 50-foot-/15-meter-high climbing plant. It needs to be kept warm in the winter, but you can put it outdoors in the summer to allow the flowers to be pollinated and grow berries.

RASPBERRY & RED CURRANT

2 glasses

2 cups/200 g raspberries

1 cup/100 g red currants

1 ripe banana

1–2 cups/100–200 ml water

1 tsp honey

Rinse the berries, remove the stalks from the currants, peel the banana, and blend all the ingredients with the water and honey until smooth.

TIP: Use 1 cup/200 ml yogurt instead of water for a delicious breakfast smoothie.

A raspberry is in fact made up of dozens of smaller berries, each containing a seed.
You should keep raspberries in the fridge, and not for more than two days.
If you put them in the freezer, they will keep for three to four months.

MIXED WILD BERRIES

2 glasses

2 apples

1 cup/100 g strawberries

1 banana

1 cup/100 g raspberries

1 cup/100 g blueberries

Wash all the fruit. Rinse the berries. Dice the apples and pass through a masticating or centrifugal juicer. Destalk the strawberries, peel the banana, and blend all the ingredients together with the apple juice until smooth.

Serve with raspberries and blueberries on a cocktail stick.

TIP: Replace the apple juice with 1½ cups/300 ml plain yogurt for a more substantial smoothie. Add honey or vanilla honey to taste (see page 98).

Raspberries grow wild on lime-free soils in northern Europe and in other parts of the world.

PEAR & GINGER

2 glasses

2 soft pears

1 inch/3 cm ginger

1 orange

½ lime

7 tbsp/100 ml water

Peel, quarter, and core the pears. Peel and grate the fresh ginger. Press the orange and lime, and make sure you discard the seeds—they add a bitter taste. Blend until thick and smooth.

TIP: Make a delicious juice by passing everything through a juicer instead. Remember to peel the lime and the orange, but not the pears, before processing them. Alternate soft and hard fruit in the machine.

In the 13th century, the medical faculty at the University of Salerno said the following about the almost magic properties of ginger: "Eat ginger and you will love and be loved like a youngster." The Portuguese took this to heart when they started to cultivate ginger in West Africa. They hoped it would do a lot of good to the "slave stock," but the effect has not been proved.

BLACKCURRANT & RED CURRANT

2 glasses

Blackcurrants:	Red currants:
2 cups/200 g blackcurrants	2 cups/200 g red currants
2 apples	2 pears
4 strawberries	½ banana
1 tsp honey	1 tsp honey

This is in fact two smoothies in one. It is as easy to serve it in layers as it is to mix the two.

Wash all the fruit and berries. Cut the apples in half and quarter the pears, remove the stalks, and dice. Juice the pears first and then the apples, but keep the two separated if you are going to make a layered smoothie. Peel and cut the banana. Destalk the strawberries.

Pour apple juice, blackcurrants, and strawberries into a beaker and blend until smooth. Add honey to taste (optional).

Pour pear juice, red currants, and banana in another beaker and blend until smooth.

Pour the blackcurrant smoothie in the glass first, then slowly spoon a red-currant layer on top. Sprinkle with blackcurrants and red currants.

TIP: ... or just blend all the ingredients.

Have you ever smelled a blackcurrant bush? It smells just as good as the berries.
You can make delicious tea or cordial from the leaves.

PAPAYA & PASSION FRUIT

2 glasses

2 apples

1 small papaya (ca. 10 oz/300 g)

1 banana

2 passion fruits

Wash the fruit. Dice the apples. Cut the papaya in half, remove the seeds, and dice the flesh. Pass the papaya and apples through a juicer, alternating papaya and apples. Transfer the juice to the blender, add passion fruit and banana, and blend quickly.

TIP: For a smoother result, remove the passion fruit seeds by pouring a little water inside the fruit, and mix it with the pulp until it the seeds separate from the pulp. Pass through a sieve and use only the liquid for the smoothie.

Nutritious papain, which relieves digestive problems, is extracted from papayas. The unripe fruit is slashed with a knife and the liquid is collected.

CRANBERRY & PEAR

2 glasses

2 cups/200 g cranberries

3 soft sweet pears

1 orange

Wash all the fruit and berries. Press the orange. Cut the pears in half, remove cores and stalks, and dice. Mix all the ingredients until thick and smooth.

TIP: Pass all the ingredients through a juicer for a less pulpy smoothie. Add a little water if it is too strong.

Just like lingonberries (cowberries) and cloudberries, cranberries contain benzoic acid, a natural preservative.

YOGURT & BREAKFAST SMOOTHIES

BLACKBERRY & VANILLA

2 glasses

½ vanilla pod

4 tsp honey

2 cups/200 g blackberries

1 cup/100 g blueberries

1½ cups/300 ml plain yogurt

3½ tbsp/50 ml water

Split the vanilla pod and scrape the seeds into a small saucepan with 3½ tbsp/50 ml water. Add the pod and boil for 2–3 minutes. Add the honey just before removing from the heat, cool, and remove the vanilla pod. Blend all the ingredients until smooth.

TIP: Make a large quantity of vanilla honey. It keeps for about 2 weeks in the fridge and can be used to flavor any type of smoothie.

According to one theory, the darker the berries, the more nutritious they are. Blackberries are the darkest of them all. They contain large amounts of potassium, which is said to protect against cancer and cardiovascular disease. Only pick ripe blackberries—they taste bad if they are picked too early. Most blackberries do not ripen until September/October.

BLACKCURRANT & QUARK

2 glasses

2 cups/200 g blackcurrants

1 cup/100 g raspberries

1 cup/200 g vanilla quark

Rinse the berries. Set aside half the currants for garnish. Mix all the other ingredients until smooth.

TIP: Use 1 cup/200 g vanilla yogurt instead of quark for variation.

Quark is made by warming soured milk and then straining it.
Quark usually has about the same fat content as yogurt and has no added salt.

VANILLA & APPLE

2 glasses

2 apples

1 cup/200 g vanilla quark cheese

½ vanilla pod

2 tsp honey

Wash and dice the apples and pass through a juicer. Split the vanilla pod and scrape out the seeds from one half. Pour apple juice, quark, and vanilla seeds into the blender and blend briefly. This type of smoothie should not be processed too long, or it will become too thin.

TIP: Use manuka honey if you can obtain it; it is delicious. Store the leftover vanilla pod in a sugar-filled jar with a tight-fitting lid.

Nothing may be added or removed for honey to be sold as honey; it must be completely "clean." Honey can be made from virtually any nectar-producing plant. Manuka honey comes from the manuka bush, which grows in New Zealand. It is considered to be especially nutritious since it contains many antioxidants that can help relieve the effects of the common cold or food poisoning, and it is said that it can be used to heal wounds.

LINGONBERRY & CARDAMOM

2 glasses

2 cups/200 g lingonberries
(cowberries)

1 banana

⅔ cup/150 g vanilla quark

1 pinch cardamom

Wash all the fruits and berries. Blend all the ingredients until smooth.

Serve with lingonberries.

TIP: If you cannot find fresh lingonberries, replace them with frozen cranberries, or try cinnamon instead of cardamom.

Lingonberries are rich in vitamin C and have been used as a source, sometimes the only source, of vitamin C in Scandinavia where they frequently accompany meatballs, black pudding, herring, and many other dishes.

OAT MILK & RASPBERRY

2 glasses

generous 2 cups/250 g raspberries

generous ¾ cup/200 ml oat milk

1 banana

Blend all the ingredients until smooth.
Pass through a sieve for an even
smoother drink.

Serve with a few raspberries.

Even the ancient Greeks recommended oatmeal porridge as an easily digested remedy for
stomach problems. The fiber is removed from oat milk for a smoother consistency.

BLUEBERRY & VANILLA

2 glasses

2 cups/200 g blueberries

1 cup/100 g raspberries

1½ cups/300 ml plain yogurt

vanilla-flavored powdered sugar

Rinse the berries and leave them to dry. Blend all the ingredients until smooth and add vanilla-flavored sugar to taste. It is delicious.

Serve with a few lemon balm leaves and sprinkle a few blueberries over the smoothie.

Vanilla was first introduced in Spain via Aztec drinking chocolate before it spread to the rest of Europe. In 1602, Queen Elizabeth I's apothecary discovered it was perfect for flavoring sweets, but it would take another 100 years for vanilla to become famous throughout Europe for a completely different reason. It was marketed as an aphrodisiac.

STRAWBERRY & LINSEED

2 glasses

3 tbsp linseed

2 cups/200 g strawberries

1 banana

1 cup/200 ml plain yogurt

Wash all the fruit. Soak the linseed or use crushed linseed. Destalk the strawberries, peel the banana, and blend until smooth and creamy.

Sprinkle with linseed.

TIP: Add some cold-pressed linseed oil for an additional energy boost.

The laxative and beneficial properties of linseed have been known since the 16th century or longer. But it is important not to overdose.

ALMOND & BANANA

2 glasses

2 bananas

1 cup/200 ml plain yogurt

2 tbsp almond butter

1 tsp vanilla-flavored powdered sugar

Peel the bananas and add yogurt, almond butter, and vanilla-flavored powdered sugar. Blend until smooth.

TIP: If you cannot find almond butter in your local health food shop, process some peeled almonds and a little water until smooth before adding the other ingredients, or use a commercial brand of almond milk.

Almond butter should not be confused with peanut butter. It is just as tasty and a lot healthier. You can make butter from other nuts too—hazelnuts, for example.

STRAWBERRY & VANILLA

2 glasses

2 cups/200 g strawberries

⅔ cup/150 g vanilla quark

3½ tbsp/50 ml milk

Destalk the strawberries. Blend with the quark and milk until smooth and fluffy. Garnish with fresh strawberries and fresh mint.

TIP: Replace the quark with yogurt and a little extra vanilla flavoring. I usually add 2 tbsp of wheat bran to keep my stomach in trim.

Fiber-rich wheat bran is an excellent breakfast cereal. It is made from the outer husk of the wheat berry, which means that it contains no gluten. However, it cannot always be absolutely guaranteed gluten free since it may be contaminated by other parts of the wheat berry.

SUMMER BERRY & YOGURT

2 glasses

1 cup/100 g strawberries

1 cup/100 g raspberries

1 cup/100 g blueberries

1½ cups/300 ml vanilla yogurt

honey

Rinse the berries and leave to dry. Blend the berries and half the yogurt until smooth. Pour the remaining yogurt into the glasses so that the white yogurt is unevenly distributed along the inside of the glass, then add the berry–yogurt mixture. You should please the eye as well as the palate. Alternatively, pour in the yogurt and berry mixture in layers.

TIP: Make your own vanilla yogurt by adding vanilla seeds, vanilla honey, vanilla syrup, or home-made vanilla-flavored powdered sugar to plain yogurt and chill. Use vanilla-flavored quark to make a dessert smoothie.

Lingonberries, blueberries, raspberries, cloudberries, and blackberries are only some of several hundred wild species.

PRUNE & CINNAMON

2 glasses

12 prunes, without pits

1½ cups/300 ml plain yogurt

1 pinch cinnamon

honey

Wash the prunes and soak for half an hour. Blend all the ingredients until smooth. Add a little honey to taste.

Serve with chopped prunes.

TIP: Vary with a few spoonfuls of goji berries for an extra vitamin boost.

Prunes are in fact dried plums. They were originally cultivated in the Syrian capital, Damascus.

VANILLA & RASPBERRY

2 glasses

½ vanilla pod
2 cups/200 g raspberries
1 cup/200 ml plain yogurt
7 tbsp/100 ml full fat milk
3 tbsp liquid honey
(preferably organic macadamia honey)
3½ tbsp/50 ml water

Split the vanilla pod down the middle and scrape the seeds into a small saucepan along with the water. Add the pod and boil for 2–3 minutes. Mix in the honey, just before removing the saucepan from the heat, cool the vanilla honey, and remove the vanilla pod. Blend all the ingredients until smooth. Dip the glasses in melted chocolate and leave to set. Pour in the smoothie.

TIP: Make a large batch of vanilla-flavored honey if you like the taste—it keeps for about two weeks in the fridge. Use it to flavor smoothies and yogurt.

Yogurt was used as far back as 2000 B.C. in the Indo-Iranian culture.
Yogurt and honey is mentioned as food for the gods.

BLACKCURRANT & OATMEAL

2 glasses

generous 2 cups/250 g blackcurrants

2 tbsp oatmeal

1 tbsp wheat bran

1 tbsp crushed linseed

1 cup/200 ml plain yogurt

3 tbsp maple syrup

Rinse the berries. Blend all the ingredients until smooth.

TIP: If blackcurrants are not in season, use frozen berries, or replace them with any other berry. You can replace the yogurt with apple juice.

White currants are exactly the same berries as red currants, but without the red pigment. There are yellow ones too. White and yellow currants are suitable for making currant wine.

VANILLA, APPLE, & HONEY

2 glasses

1 cup/200 ml plain yogurt

1 cup/200 ml Greek yogurt

1 apple

½ vanilla pod

3 tbsp liquid honey
(preferably acacia honey)

3½ tbsp/50 ml water

Wash and cut the apple in half, peel, remove the core, and dice. Split the vanilla pod down the middle and scrape the seeds into a small saucepan with the water and the apple chunks. Add the vanilla pod and boil for 2–3 minutes. Mix in the honey just before removing the saucepan from the heat, cool the vanilla honey, and remove the vanilla pod. Blend all the ingredients until smooth. Refrigerate quickly before serving to bring out the vanilla and honey flavors.

TIP: Omit the Greek yogurt for a more liquid smoothie.

The Mexican Totona tribe have a story about the fertility goddess Xanath, who fell in love with a mortal man. She turned herself into a vanilla orchid in order to be close to him. This was how vanilla came to be. The Totona learned how to use vanilla, and later the Spaniards picked it up from the Aztecs.

VEGETABLE SMOOTHIES

CARROT & PINEAPPLE

2 glasses

6 carrots (1¼ cup/300 ml fresh
carrot juice)

½ pineapple

½ lime

4 ice cubes

Wash and brush the carrots and pass
through a juicer. Refrigerate the carrot
juice, which tastes best cold. Wash
and cut the pineapple in half, remove
the leaves, peel, and remove the tough
center. Place the pineapple flesh, carrot juice, and ice in a blender. Cut the
lime in half and squeeze out the juice.
Be sure to discard the seeds—they
add a bitter taste. Blend until smooth.

Serve with a slice of pineapple or carrots.

TIP: Pass all the ingredients through
a juicer if you prefer a more liquid
mixture. Leftover pineapple can be
kept in an airtight plastic bag in the
freezer.

Carrots are the most vitamin rich of all vegetables. They are best kept without their tops in a plastic
bag in the fridge or in a cool larder. The carrot tops leach nutrients from the carrots.

CUCUMBER, APPLE, & LIME

2 glasses

1 cucumber

3 apples

½ lime

Wash all the fruit and the cucumber. Peel and slice the cucumber. Cut the apples in half, and remove the stalks and seeds—they add a bitter taste to the smoothie. Dice the apples. Alternate cucumber and apples in the juicer. Squeeze the juice from the lime straight into the glass.

Serve with apple and cucumber slices.

TIP: Vary by adding celery or wheatgrass.

The cucumber originated in India. It is in fact a fruit. It contains as much as 96% water. Because of its mild taste, many think it lacks nutrients, but it does contain vitamin C.

BEET & CHILLI

2 glasses

2 raw mini beets

2 apples

½ red chilli

Wash and brush the beets, apples, and chilli carefully. Dice the beets and apples. Remove the seeds and membranes from the chilli unless you want it really spicy. Process all the ingredients through a juicer. Cool with plenty of ice in a large shaker or stir with ice in the glass. Serve immediately.

TIP: Clean the juicer from chilli or other strong-tasting ingredients by immediately afterwards juicing a lemon (without the pith). It removes the strong flavors naturally. You still need to wash the juicer in order to save a great deal of trouble later.

Small beets are easier to handle since you do not need to cut them and thereby stain your cutting board. Remember that beet greens are very nutritious. Save them and make a beet soup with the greens.

AVOCADO & MANGO

2 glasses

2 avocados

1 mango

½ lemon

generous ¾ cup/200 ml water

Cut the avocado in half, remove the pit, and scoop out the flesh with a spoon. Peel the mango and dice— remember there is a large pit inside. Cut the lemon in half and squeeze out the juice into the mixer. Make sure you do not include the seeds; they add a bitter taste to the smoothie. Blend until smooth and creamy.

TIP: If you have to keep half an avocado, leave the pit inside, squeeze a little lemon over the surface, and cover in plastic wrap. Refrigerate and eat within 24 hours.

Mango is the national fruit of India and Pakistan. It contains many nutrients, including carotene and antioxidants, but also urushiol, which is found in cashew nuts too. People who are allergic to nuts should be cautious, at least when handling the skin.

PEAR, KIWI, & BROCCOLI

2 glasses

2 pears

1 apple

2 kiwis

½ banana

5 broccoli florets

Wash all the fruit and broccoli. Cut the apple and pears in half, remove the stalks, and dice. Break off a few broccoli florets. Put the apples, pears, and broccoli alternately in a juicer.
Peel the banana and kiwi. Pour the juice into the blender and blend with the kiwi and banana, but not too long since the kiwi seeds may break and add a bitter taste to the smoothie.

TIP: Start with a small amount of broccoli if you are unsure whether you like it or not. I was surprised to find how well it went with the rest of the ingredients, but you should go easy on it.

Broccoli comes from Italy. The name derives from *brocco*, an Italian word meaning "fragile branch."

BEET & CARROT

2 glasses

3 raw mini beets
5 carrots
3 tart green apples
(e.g. Granny Smith)

Brush and wash the beets, carrots, and apples carefully. Dice everything and put through a juicer. Serve immediately on ice in a large glass.

TIP: Add a celery stalk for an extra vitamin boost.

Carrots contain plenty of beta-carotene, which forms vitamin A in the body. The so-called mini or baby carrot is a peeled carrot that has been cut into bite-size pieces. It was produced as a healthy alternative to fries in fast food restaurants. Carrots are healthy food, but not—which you often hear—a cure for bad eyesight. This myth derives from the fact that the lack of vitamin A can affect your sight.

STRAWBERRY & BEET

2 glasses

¼ raw mini beet

½ lime

2 cups/200 g strawberries

1 cup/200 ml vanilla yogurt

Brush and wash the beet, rinse the berries and lime. Peel and grate the beet finely or pass it through a juicer. Press the lime with a citrus press and pour the fresh juice into the blender. Destalk the strawberries and blend everything until smooth.

TIP: The beet adds a very interesting flavor. It is full of antioxidants and adds a lovely color to this smoothie.

Beets contain calcium, vitamin C, iron, magnesium, phosphorus, and manganese. They are also said to cleanse the liver and gut, and aid kidney function.

CARROT, ORANGE, & CHILLI

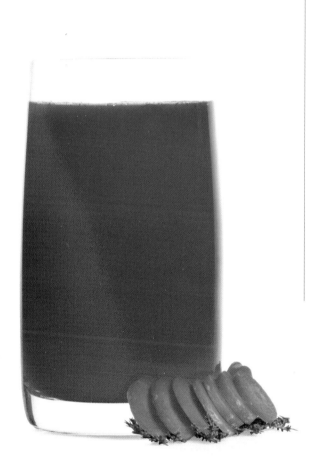

2 glasses

6 carrots

2 oranges

½ red chilli

Scrub and wash all the fruit ingredients in lukewarm water. It is important to wash the citrus fruits in order to prevent any pesticide residues entering the smoothie. Peel the carrots if necessary and slice. Peel and cut the oranges. Cut the chilli in half lengthways and remove the seeds. Alternate chilli, carrots, and orange in the juicer.

Serve immediately with slices of carrot on the side, or strips of chilli for the more adventurous.

TIP: When you need to clean the juicer from chilli or other strong tastes, juice a lemon (without the pith) immediately after you have used it. It removes the strong flavors naturally.

You can become addicted to chilli because of capsaicin, which stimulates endorphin production in the body. Endorphins make you relaxed and relieve pain, so it is not strange if you long for a bit of chilli every now and then.

BEET & GARLIC

2 glasses

2 raw mini beets

2 apples

2 garlic cloves

½ lime

2 tsp honey

Rinse the fruit and vegetables. Peel the garlic cloves. Peel and cut up the lime. Dice the apples and beets, discarding the peel and core. Juice the beets, lime, garlic, and apples. Pour 1 tsp honey into the bottom of each glass, pour on the juice and serve immediately.

TIP: Just add more garlic if you have got a cold. It may not taste very nice, but honey and garlic are supposed to work. At least it can't hurt …

Fresh garlic is a little milder than garlic salt.
Fresh garlic may increase fat metabolism and reduce sugar craving.

AVOCADO & PINEAPPLE

2 glasses

½ pineapple

1 avocado

½ lime

7 tbsp/100 ml water

Cut the pineapple in half, remove the leaves and peel. Dice and pass through a juicer (or use readymade juice). Cut the avocado in half, remove the pit, and scoop out the flesh with a spoon. Add lime juice. Blend until thick and smooth.

TIP: Juice the pineapple before you mix in the avocado for a more liquid smoothie.

Find a ripe pineapple by trying to pull out one of the leaves at the bottom. It will come out easily if the pineapple is ripe, but it may be overripe. It is wiser to choose one that is not quite ripe and keep it for a few days at home.

AVOCADO & SPINACH

2 glasses

3 green apples

2 avocados

1 lime

1 cup/50 g baby spinach

Wash all the fruit well. Peel, quarter, and core the apples. Pass the apple chunks through a juicer. Cut the avocados in half, remove the pits, and use a spoon to scoop out the flesh. Cut the lime in half and squeeze the juice straight into the blender, but make sure that no seeds are included—they add a bitter taste. Blend until smooth.

Garnish with baby spinach.

TIP: Use good-quality, freshly-made apple juice if you do not have time to make your own.

Avocado is a berry named after the Spanish *aguacate*, which in turn comes from the Aztec word *ahuacatl*, which means "testicle" (referring to the shape). Throughout the ages, avocado has been considered an aphrodisiac. Apart from the alleged potency-enhancing properties and the fatty acids, avocados have many other good properties. It is an old herbal remedy used externally to improve skin and hair.

BEET & CELERY

2 glasses

2 raw mini beets

2 carrots

1 apple

1 stalk of celery

½ lime

Wash and scrub the vegetables and fruit well. Peel the lime, carrots, apple, and celery. Pass everything through a juicer. Cool in a large shaker filled with ice or stir until chilled in a glass. Serve immediately.

The myth that carrots are good for the eyesight may derive from the claim that British Royal Air Force pilots during WWII gained better night vision from eating carrots. They suddenly seemed to hit more targets than they did before they started eating carrots. But the truth is probably that the reason was the advent of radar.

DESSERT SMOOTHIES

CHOCOLATE & MINT

2 glasses

4 scoops of good-quality ice cream

generous ¾ cup/200 ml milk

⅓ cup/50 g dark chocolate chips

a few drops of mint extract

Melt the chocolate in warm milk and leave to cool. Blend all the ingredients until smooth.

Serve with chocolate and mint.

TIP: If you happen to have a box of After Eights at home, you can use those or replace the ice cream with mint chocolate ice cream.

The cocoa fruit resembles an 8-inch/20-cm-long cucumber and contains almond-size seeds. The seeds are fermented and toasted and then crushed and ground to a paste, from which "cocoa butter" is made. When the fat has been pressed out of the beans, the residue is pulverized to make cocoa powder.

CHERRY & COCONUT

2 glasses

2 cups/200 g cherries

⅔ cup/150 g vanilla quark

3 tbsp coconut milk

honey

Wash the cherries and remove the pits. Blend the cherries, quark, and coconut milk until smooth. Add honey to taste.

TIP: Since cherries can be hard to find, you can use frozen cherries instead. Decorate the glass by dipping it in chocolate for an attractive visual effect. Or garnish with home-made chocolate figures.

If you can get them, use "sweet cherries." The sweet cherry is a firmer, less juicy sub-species of the cherry.

CHOCOLATE & BANANA

2 glasses

2 bananas

3 scoops vanilla ice cream

7 tbsp/100 ml milk

2 tsp cocoa powder

vanilla-flavored powdered sugar

Wash and peel the bananas. Blend all the ingredients until smooth.

TIP: Bananas freeze well in resealable plastic bags. Use them when you are out of fresh ones.

Chocolate with high cocoa content has become fashionable, and the percentage is sometimes printed on the packaging. Cocoa contains antioxidants, vitamins, and minerals and is supposed to be good for the heart. Apart from the cocoa, white chocolate contains exactly the same ingredients as brown chocolate.

WHITE CHOCOLATE & RASPBERRIES

2 glasses

⅓ cup/50 g white chocolate chips

4 scoops of vanilla ice cream

2 cups/200 g raspberries

3 tbsp milk

Powder the chocolate in the blender. Add milk, raspberries, and vanilla ice cream and blend until smooth.

TIP: The best ice cream is homemade. If you do use a commercial brand, use a good-quality one made from real vanilla and cream. Read the list of contents to make sure there are no unnecessary additives.

White chocolate contains no cocoa powder.
The rest of the ingredients are identical to those in brown chocolate.

COFFEE & VANILLA

2 glasses

5 scoops of vanilla ice cream

¾ cup/200 ml milk

⅓ cup/100 ml cold espresso or strong coffee

grated chocolate for garnish

Make a delicious milkshake smoothie by blending all the ingredients. Sprinkle with grated chocolate.

TIP: Add more coffee if you like the taste. Serve with a few coffee beans.

The word "coffee" comes from Arabic and means wine. When wine was banned in Muslim countries, coffee took its place as a social beverage.

CHOCOLATE & CHILLI

2 glasses

1¼ cups/300 ml milk

3 scoops of ice cream

⅓ cup/50 g dark chocolate chips

¼ red chilli

Heat the milk and add the chocolate. Stir until it has melted. Add 2–4 slices of chilli without the seeds and refrigerate. Remove the chilli slices before adding the ice cream. Blend until smooth. Garnish with chocolate twists. You make them by gently "peeling" the edge of the chocolate with a potato peeler.

TIP: Chocolate and chilli is a great combo, but if you are not used to strong flavors, start with one or two slices of chilli.

If you are suffering from a sore throat, make a soothing hot infusion by mixing ½ tsp cinnamon with 1 tsp chopped, fresh ginger and ¼ tsp chopped red chilli. Sweeten with a little honey and add lemon or lime juice. It has been suggested that chilli aids weight reduction since it increases body temperature and thus the metabolic rate.

CHOCOLATE & VANILLA

2 glasses

1 cup/200 g vanilla quark

½ cup/100 ml plain yogurt

⅓ cup/50 g dark chocolate chips

2 tbsp water

Melt the chocolate in a bain-marie and mix in 2 tbsp hot water. Add 3 tbsp quark to prevent it from setting. Blend the chocolate cream with the other ingredients. For a pretty smoothie trickle chocolate cream on the inside of the glass, pour in the white mixture, and drizzle chocolate cream on top.

TIP: If you like mint chocolate, add a couple of drops of mint extract to the cream or melt two After Eight wafers with the rest of the chocolate.

Vanilla derives from the Latin word vagina (because of the sheath-like vanilla pod).
Perhaps this was enough to inspire the German doctor Bezaar Zimmeran in the 18th century
to claim that vanilla was unequaled as an aphrodisiac and a cure for impotence.

HAZELNUT & CHOCOLATE

2 glasses

⅔ cup/100 g hazelnuts

⅓ cup/50 g dark chocolate chips

1 banana

⅔ cup/150 g vanilla ice cream

generous ¾ cup/200 ml milk

Powder the hazelnuts and dark chocolate. Peel the banana. Add the milk and banana, and blend until smooth. Blend in the ice cream.

Pour into glasses and drizzle a little melted chocolate or chocolate sauce on top.

TIP: Health food shops sell 100% pure hazelnut paste that can be used instead of ground hazelnuts.

The nutritious hazelnut has been appreciated and cultivated ever since the Middle Ages. These days they are often added to cakes and pastries.

COCONUT & CHOCOLATE

2 glasses

⅓ cup/50 g dark chocolate chips

7 tbsp/100 ml milk

1 banana

2 tbsp coconut milk

⅔ cup/150 g vanilla ice cream

fresh or shredded coconut

Melt the chocolate in warm milk and leave to cool. Peel the banana. Add coconut milk and ice cream, and blend until smooth. Grate a little fresh coconut on top, or use desiccated, shredded coconut.

Serve with fresh coconut on the side.

TIP: Always buy good-quality chocolate with a minimum cocoa content of 50% and make sure there are no unnecessary additives in the coconut milk and ice cream.

How do you break open a coconut? Prick a hole in each of the three "eyes" at one end and pour out the liquid. Place the nut in a 400 °F/200 °C oven for 20 minutes. Use the back of a large knife to tap round the middle of the nut. The shell will crack and break easily. Peel off the thin, brown layer with a potato peeler.

POMEGRANATE & COCONUT

2 glasses

½ pomegranate

2 cups/200 g strawberries

⅔ cup/150 g vanilla quark

7 tbsp/100 ml coconut milk or cream

2 tsp coconut flakes

Wash the pomegranate and strawberries. Destalk the strawberries. Cut the pomegranate in half and extract the juice using a citrus press. Pour all the ingredients into a blender and blend until smooth.

Serve with a few pomegranate seeds.

TIP: Mix the smoothie with a few cubes of crushed ice to make a frozen smoothie.

The pomegranate has biblical roots. The First Book of Kings describes how the capitals of the pillars in King Soloman's temple were in the form of pomegranates. Pomegranates are also mentioned in the Song of Songs, where the fruit is compared to the beauty of a woman. The seeds are fertility symbols.

FRUITY COCKTAILS

STRAWBERRY MARGARITA

¼ cup/60 ml tequila

3 tbsp/45 ml lemon juice

1 tbsp/15 ml corn syrup

6 fresh strawberries

1 lemon wedge

Pour all the ingredients except the lime into a blender with crushed ice and mix them until half frozen—stop before they turn into sorbet. Pour into a cocktail glass with a frosted rim.

Frosted Rim: Pour salt or sugar onto a saucer. Moisten the rim of the glass with the lime wedge and dip the upturned glass into the contents of the saucer.

Tequila must contain at least 51% agave to be allowed the name tequila. The most exclusive tequila is made with 100% agave and aged in oak barrels. However, don't use this sort of tequila for cocktails— it's better to drink it like a fine Scotch.

FROZEN MOJITO

¼ cup/60 ml light rum

2 tbsp/30 ml lime juice

1 tbsp/15 ml corn syrup

6–10 mint leaves

crushed ice

Pour all the ingredients into a blender. Blend briefly at high speed until smooth. Add crushed ice—start with a small amount and add more until you get the desired thickness. Serve in a cocktail glass.

Mojito was one of Ernest Hemingway's favourite drinks during his time in Cuba. He used to enjoy them at La Bodeguita del Medio in Havana. The author is part of the reason why this Cuban drink has become so successful worldwide. This is the frozen form, which is almost as famous as the original. (The more mint leaves, the greener the Mojito.)

FROZEN BLACKBERRY DAIQUIRI

3 tbsp/45 ml golden rum

1 tbsp/15 ml Crème de Mûre

5 blackberries

2 tbsp/30 ml lemon juice

1 tbsp/15 ml honey

crushed ice

Pour all the ingredients into a blender. Blend briefly at high speed until smooth. Add crushed ice—start with a small amount and add more until you achieve the desired thickness. Serve in a margarita glass and garnish with lemon balm.

Frozen Daiquiri is a common Daiquiri variation . Besides rum, lime juice, and corn syrup, it contains crushed ice and fruit or berries. For a more intense flavor, add a matching liqueur, as we have here.

FROZEN BLUEBERRY DAIQUIRI

2 tbsp/30 ml light rum

2 tbsp/30 ml blueberry liqueur

¼ cup/60 ml blueberries

2 tbsp/30 ml lime juice

1 tbsp/15 ml corn syrup

crushed ice

Pour all the ingredients into a blender. Blend briefly at high speed until smooth. Add crushed ice—start with a small amount and add more until you achieve the desired thickness. Serve in a margarita glass and garnish with lemon balm.

TIP! You can also try using home-made or a commercial brand of blueberry purée.

Nordic forest fruits meet the national spirit of Cuba to celebrate the summer.

FROZEN BANANA DAIQUIRI

¼ cup/60 ml light rum

½ banana

2 tbsp/30 ml lime or lemon juice

1 tbsp/15 ml corn syrup

crushed ice

Pour all the ingredients into a blender. Blend briefly at high speed until smooth. Add crushed ice—start with a small amount and add more until you achieve the desired thickness. Serve in a margarita glass.

Daiquiri comes in a million versions over and above the original cocktail of rum, citrus, and sugar. Legendary bartender Constante made the Floridita restaurant famous with his own version made with maraschino liqueur and crushed ice. For Hemingway he added grapefruit juice instead of sugar. Until this day, tourists and Cubans go on pilgrimages to the Floridita bar, where Daiquiris are said to taste better than anywhere else in the world.

FROZEN RASPBERRY DAIQUIRI

¼ cup/60 ml Bacardi Razz

8–10 raspberries

2 tbsp/30 ml lime juice

1 tbsp/15 ml corn syrup

crushed ice

Pour all the ingredients into a blender. Blend briefly at high speed until smooth. Add crushed ice— start with a small amount and add more until you achieve the desired thickness. Serve in a margarita glass and garnish with fresh raspberries.

The trick of mixing a perfect original Daiquiri is to squeeze the lime gently to avoid adding the bitter juice from the peel. Blend the drink for a few seconds only, no longer. If you're not very experienced, you can mix a flavored Daiquiri instead, like the one on page 147, which is made with raspberries.
You can't go wrong, and it's incredibly tasty!

FROZEN CHI CHI

¼ cup/60 ml vodka

2 tbsp/30 ml thick coconut cream

3 tbsp/45 ml pineapple juice

crushed ice

Pour all the ingredients into a blender. Blend briefly at high speed until smooth. Add crushed ice—start with a small amount and add more until you achieve the desired thickness. Pour into a glass of your choice and garnish with a tropical touch.

TIP! If you are not a fan of coconut cream, try coconut liqueur or coconut syrup instead. Add half a banana for the right thickness.

Blue Hawaii made with curaçao and Chi Chi made with vodka are both Piña Colada variations.

RASPBERRY KISS

2 tbsp/30 ml white crème de cacao

2 tbsp/30 ml raspberry liqueur

2 tbsp/30 ml heavy cream

crushed ice

Pour all the ingredients into a blender. Blend briefly at high speed until smooth. Add crushed ice—start with a small amount and add more until you achieve the desired thickness. Pour into a glass of your choice and garnish with fresh raspberries.

Raspberries grow wild all over northern Europe, and they are also cultivated commercially all year round. They are to be found where the landscape is a bit rocky and round forest clearings, which is where raspberry bushes thrive.

FROZEN MANGO SLING

3 tbsp/45 ml Absolut Apeach

1 tbsp/15 ml peach liqueur

1 tbsp/15 ml lemon juice

1 tbsp/15 ml corn syrup

1 diced mango

crushed ice

Pour all the ingredients into a blender. Blend briefly at high speed until smooth. Add crushed ice—start with a small amount and add more until you achieve the desired thickness. Serve in a highball glass and garnish with fresh mango.

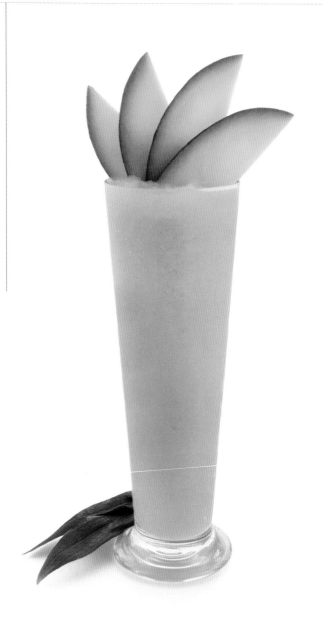

According to the Guinness Book of World Records, the world's heaviest mango weighed 7 lb 11 oz/3.5 kg. It was presented by Sergio and Maria Socorro Bodiongan at the Sundayag Celebration's Pinaka Contest in Cagayan de Oro City, Philippines, on 27 August 2009.

BLACKBERRY BEAST

3 tbsp/45 ml absinthe

1 tbsp/15 ml Crème de Mûre

2 tbsp/30 ml cranberry juice

6 mint leaves

5 blackberries

2 tbsp blueberry puree

1 tsp demerara sugar

champagne

Muddle the blackberries, mint leaves, and sugar in a shaker. Fill up with a scoop of crushed ice and add absinthe, Crème de Mûre, purée, and cranberry juice. Shake well. Strain into a highball glass and fill up with more crushed ice. Top with champagne and stir gently. Garnish with mixed berries.

Judging by the long list of ingredients, this mixture may appear slightly mad. And what about the absinthe? Doesn't it drive you insane? No, research shows that the old recipe contained only harmless amounts of the toxin, which suggests that the monstrous effects noted were due to nothing but sheer drunkenness. This cocktail is indeed a bit of a beast, but definitely worth the trouble!

FROZEN PEACH DAIQUIRI

¼ cup/60 ml light rum

3 tbsp/45 ml peach puree

2 tbsp/30 ml lime juice

1 tbsp/15 ml corn syrup

crushed ice

Pour all the ingredients into a blender. Blend briefly at high speed until smooth. Add crushed ice—start with a small amount and add more until you achieve the desired thickness. Serve in a margarita glass.

TIP! For a more intense peach flavor, replace the corn syrup with peach juice.

Christopher Columbus brought the first sugar canes from Asia to Cuba in the 15th century—which is good for us, because it's impossible to produce rum without sugar.

BLOODY MARY

¼ cup/60 ml vodka

1 dash Worcestershire sauce

¼ tsp salt

¼ tsp pepper

1 tbsp/15 ml lemon juice

2 dashes Tabasco

tomato juice

celery stick for garnish

Pour the first six ingredients into an ice-filled highball glass. Fill up with tomato juice and stir. Garnish with a celery stick.

Best known as the world's number 1 hangover cure—perhaps due to its saltiness. Many believe that this cocktail was named after Mary I, the bloodthirsty queen of England who was known for her many executions. A more likely story involves Pete Petiot, bartender at Harry's New York Bar in Paris and a Mary Pickford fan. Mary Pickford was a silent movie star known as "the whole world's little sweetheart." "Bloody" would then refer to the drink's color.

THAI MOJITO

¼ cup/60 ml Havana Club Añejo
Reserva

½ lime

1 tsp demerara sugar

1 tbsp/15 ml ginger juice

6 cilantro leaves

1 chilli for garnish

Muddle the lime, cilantro, sugar,
and half of the chilli in a tumbler. Fill
up the glass with crushed ice, add
rum, and stir. Serve with a straw and
garnish with chilli and cilantro leaves.

Fresh grated ginger is used in much the same way as dried ginger, but it is juicier and crisper.
Ginger was first brought to northern Europe by the Romans, and it was one of the most popular
spices of the Middle Ages.

SANGRIA

Serves 10–15

2 bottles sweet Spanish red wine

½ cup/120 ml Cointreau

6 tbsp/90 ml brandy

6 tbsp/90 ml orange juice

¼ cup/60 ml lemon juice

¼ cup/60 ml lime juice

1 cup/240 ml corn syrup

orange slices

lemon slices

lime slices

grapes

Pour all the liquid ingredients into a large bowl (or two pitchers) and give everything a good stir. Add 1 pint/ 500 ml of ice cubes and the fruit.

TIP! Sangria is a type of Spanish punch to which all sorts of fruits and berries can be added. Try replacing the oranges with peaches. Why not add a few cups of iced black tea? Instead of juices, you can use various soft drinks, and you can vary the strength and intensity by increasing or decreasing the amount of brandy. Brandy can be excluded altogether or replaced with vodka.

The word "Sangria" comes from *sangre,* the Spanish word for "blood," probably because of the blood-red color of this popular party punch. It is the perfect drink for a summer event. It is deliciously refreshing, but be careful—it is a lot stronger than the sweet taste leads you to believe …

STRAWBERRY COLADA

3 tbsp/45 ml white rum

1 tbsp/15 ml strawberry liqueur

3 tbsp/45 ml thick coconut milk

¼ cup/60 ml pineapple juice

1 tbsp/15 ml heavy cream

4 strawberries + 1 for garnish

crushed ice

Pour the ingredients into a blender. Blend briefly at high speed until smooth. Pour into an exotic hurricane glass and garnish with fresh strawberries.

In general, women have more taste buds on their tongues than men, which normally makes them more sensitive to strong and intense flavors. The difference can be enormous—one person can have 11 taste buds—and someone else 1,100 in the same small area! There are, of course, individual differences, but this could be a reason why women are often prone to liking sweet and fruity "girly drinks" such as this ...

STRAWBERRY DAIQUIRI

¼ cup/60 ml light rum

4–6 strawberries

2 tbsp/30 ml lime juice

1 tbsp/15 ml corn syrup

crushed ice

Pour all the ingredients into a blender. Blend briefly at high speed until smooth. Add crushed ice—start with a small amount and add more until you achieve the desired thickness. Serve in a margarita glass and garnish with fresh strawberries.

Almost as well known as the original, Frozen Strawberry Daiquiri is simply a must in the summer.
It's bound to seduce just about anyone ...

ACKNOWLEDGMENTS

I would like to thank my dear husband and agent, **Stefan Lindström**, who always believes in me and my crazy ideas. I appreciate our long and uplifting discussions that have brought me new ideas and fresh inspiration. I also want to thank you for tasting and judging every recipe found in this book. I would also like to thank my dear brother **Alan Maranik** for the beautiful design—working with you is always an inspiration, and my dear sister **Adriana Maranik** for her help with adapting the translated text to the layout.

I would also like to thank **Sara Hallström** who did the research—you are a gem! My editor **Rebecka Wolff** for her fantastic input and **Katarina Trodden** for translating the book into English. Thank you **Roland Glukhov**, who helped me during photo sessions and post-processing, and many thanks to **Tony Greenwood** and **Hannah Jarvis Howard** at Massolit, London, and the **Turnaround** sales team. And, finally, I would like to thank the **Marriott Marbella Beach Resort** and the **Key West Marriott Beachside Hotel** for being such inspirational and wonderful places for a writer.

Eliq Maranik

INDEX

Mango
  Avocado & Mango 117
  Frozen Mango Sling 148
  Kiwi & Mango 65
  Mandarin & Mango 51
  Mango & Chilli 56
  Mango & Ginger 63
  Mango & Lemon Balm 66
  Mango & Passion Fruit 40
  Mango & Pineapple 76
  Mango & Rosehip 48
  Mango & Strawberry 46
  Nectarine & Mango 80
  Orange & Mango 37
  Orange, Mango, &
  Pomegranate 41
  Raspberry & Mango 68
  Red Currant & Mango 59
Melon
  Blueberry & Melon 53
  Melon & Banana 81
  Melon & Goji Berries 85
  Melon & Passion Fruit 79
  Melon & Raspberry 70
Mint
  Chocolate & Mint 128
  Watermelon, Raspberry, & Mint 36
Mixed Wild Berries 91
Mojito
  Frozen Mojito 141
  Thai Mojito 152
Nectarine
  Nectarine & Mango 80
  Nectarine & Raspberry 34
Oat Milk & Raspberry 102
Oatmeal
  Blackcurrant & Oatmeal 110
Orange
  Apricot & Orange 44
  Carrot, Orange & Chilli 121
  Kiwi & Orange 77
  Orange & Banana 60
  Orange & Mango 37
  Orange, Mango, &
  Pomegranate 41
Papaya
  Mandarin & Papaya 73
  Papaya & Mandarin 82
  Papaya & Passion Fruit 94
Passion Fruit
  Banana & Passion Fruit 47

Mango & Passion Fruit 40
Melon & Passion Fruit 79
Papaya & Passion Fruit 94
Pear & Passion Fruit 89
Raspberry & Passion Fruit 38
Peach
  Frozen Peach Daiquiri 150
  Peach & Raspberry 84
Pear
  Cranberry & Pear 95
  Pear & Ginger 92
  Pear, Kiwi, & Broccoli 118
  Pear & Passion Fruit 89
  Raspberry & Pear 55
Pineapple
  Apple, Pineapple, & Ginger 86
  Avocado & Pineapple 123
  Carrot & Pineapple 114
  Coconut & Pineapple 67
  Mango & Pineapple 76
  Pineapple & Lemon Balm 42
  Strawberry & Pineapple 64
Plum & Rosehip 88
Pomegranate
  Orange, Mango, &
  Pomegranate 41
  Pomegranate & Coconut 137
  Pomegranate & Grapefruit 57
  Pomegranate & Watermelon 71
Prune
  Prune & Almond 75
  Prune & Cinnamon 108
Quark
  Blackcurrant & Quark 99
Raspberry
  Blackcurrant & Raspberry 35
  Frozen Raspberry Daiquiri 145
  Melon & Raspberry 70
  Nectarine & Raspberry 34
  Oat Milk & Raspberry 102
  Peach & Raspberry 84
  Raspberry & Red Currant 90
  Raspberry & Blueberry 61
  Raspberry Kiss 147
  Raspberry & Mango 68
  Raspberry & Passion Fruit 38
  Raspberry & Pear 55
  Vanilla & Raspberry 109
  Watermelon, Raspberry, &
  Mint 36
  White Chocolate & Raspberries 131

Red Currant
  Blackcurrant & Red Currant 93
  Raspberry & Red Currant 90
  Red currant & Mango 59
Rhubarb & Strawberry 83
Rosehip
  Mango & Rosehip 48
  Plum & Rosehip 88
Spinach
  Avocado & Spinach 124
Strawberry
  Açai & Strawberry 43
  Blackcurrant & Strawberry 87
  Grapefruit & Strawberry 52
  Mango & Strawberry 46
  Rhubarb & Strawberry 83
  Strawberry & Banana 78
  Strawberry & Basil 54
  Strawberry & Beet 120
  Strawberry & Chilli 50
  Strawberry Colada 154
  Strawberry Daiquiri 155
  Strawberry & Linseed 104
  Strawberry Margarita 140
  Strawberry & Pineapple 64
  Strawberry & Vanilla 106
  Watermelon, Strawberry, &
  Lime 74
Summer Berry & Yogurt 107
Vanilla
  Blackberry & Vanilla 98
  Blueberry & Vanilla 103
  Chocolate & Vanilla 134
  Coffee & Vanilla 132
  Strawberry & Vanilla 106
  Vanilla & Apple 100
  Vanilla, Apple, & Honey 111
  Vanilla & Raspberry 109
Watermelon
  Pomegranate & Watermelon 71
  Watermelon, Raspberry, &
  Mint 36
  Watermelon, Strawberry, &
  Lime 74
White Chocolate & Raspberries 131
Wild Berries
  Mixed Wild Berries 91
Yogurt
  Summer Berry & Yogurt 107

Abbreviations and Quantities

1 oz = 1 ounce = 28 grams
1 lb = 1 pound = 16 ounces
1 cup = approx. 5–8 ounces* (see below)
1 cup = 8 fluid ounces = 250 milliliters (liquids)
2 cups = 1 pint (liquids)
8 pints = 4 quarts = 1 gallon (liquids)
1 g = 1 gram = 1/1000 kilogram = 5 ml (liquids)
1 kg = 1 kilogram = 1000 grams = 2¼ lb
1 l = 1 liter = 1000 milliliters (ml) = 1 quart
125 milliliters (ml) = approx. 8 tablespoons = ½ cup
1 tbsp = 1 level tablespoon = 15–20 g* (depending on density) = 15 milliliters (liquids)
1 tsp = 1 level teaspoon = 3–5 g* (depending on density) = 5 ml (liquids)

*The weight of dry ingredients varies significantly depending on the density factor, e.g. 1 cup of flour weighs less than 1 cup of butter. Quantities in ingredients have been rounded up or down for convenience, where appropriate. Metric conversions may therefore not correspond exactly. It is important to use either American or metric measurements within a recipe.

© of the original edition:
Eliq Maranik and Stevali Production

Original title:
Smoothies – förföriska fruktfantasier för alla smaker!
ISBN 978-91-86287-13-9

Product idea, smoothies, and styling: Eliq Maranik
Art Director: Eliq Maranik / Stevali Production
Graphic design and illustrations: Alan Maranik and Eliq Maranik / Stevali Production

All photos by Eliq Maranik / Stevali Production, except:
p. 16, 20, 22, 28, 32, 96, 112, 126, 138–iStockphoto

© of this English edition:
h.f.ullmann publishing GmbH

Translated from the Swedish by Katarina Trodden
Project management for h.f.ullmann publishing: Isabel Weiler
Americanization: First Edition Translations Ltd, Cambridge, UK
Cover design: Simone Sticker
Overall responsibility for production: h.f.ullmann publishing GmbH, Potsdam, Germany

Printed in China, 2013

ISBN 978-3-8480-0285-6

10 9 8 7 6 5 4 3 2 1
X IX VIII VII VI V IV III II I

www.ullmann-publishing.com
newsletter@ullmann-publishing.com